THE RACE QUESTION IN MODERN SCIENCE

THE RACE CONCEPT

Results of an Inquiry

GREENWOOD PRESS, PUBLISHERS
WESTPORT, CONNECTICUT

CONTENTS

Since the beginning of the nineteenth century, the racial problem has been growing in importance A bare 30 years ago, Europeans could still regard race prejudice as a phenomenon that only affected areas on the margin of civilization, or continents other than their own. They suffered a sudden and rude awakening. The long-standing confusion between race and culture has produced fertile soil for the development of racism, at once a creed and an emotional attitude. The virulence with which this ideology has made its appearance during the present century is one of the strangest and most disturbing phenomena of the great revolution of our time. Racial doctrine is the outcome of a fundamentally anti-rational system of thought and is in glaring conflict with the whole humanist tradition of our civilization. It sets at nought everything that Unesco stands for and endeavours to defend. By virtue of its very constitution, Unesco must face the racial problem: the preamble to that document declares that "the great and terrible war which has now ended was a war made possible by the denial of the democratic principles of the dignity, equality and mutual respect of men, and by the propagation, in their place, through ignorance and prejudice, of the doctrine of the inequality of men and races".

Because of its structure and the tasks assigned to it, Unesco is the international institution best equipped to lead the campaign against race prejudice and to extirpate this most dangerous of doctrines. Race hatred and conflict thrive on scientifically false ideas and are nourished by ignorance. In order to show up these errors of fact and reasoning, to make widely known the conclusions reached in various branches of science, to combat racial propaganda, we must turn to the means and methods of education, science and culture, which are precisely the three domains in which Unesco's activities are exerted; it is on this threefold front that the battle against all forms of racism must be engaged.

The plan laid down by the Organization proceeds from a resolution [116 (VI) B. (iii)] adopted by the United Nations Economic and Social Council at its Sixth Session, asking Unesco "to consider the desirability of initiating and recommending the general adoption of a programme of disseminating scientific facts designed to remove what is generally known as racial prejudice".

Responding to this request, the Fourth Session of Unesco's General Conference adopted the following three resolutions for the 1950 programme: "The Director-General is instructed: to study and collect scientific materials concerning questions of race; to give wide diffusion to the scientific information collected; to prepare an educational campaign based on this information."

Such a programme could not be carried out unless Unesco had at its disposal the "scientific facts" mentioned in the resolution of the Economic and Social Council. For the purpose of securing these facts with as little delay as possible, the Department of Social Sciences, at that time under Dr. Arthur Ramos, convened a committee of anthropologists, psychologists and sociologists, whose task was to define the concept of race and to give an account in "clear and easily understandable" terms of our present knowledge regarding the highly controversial problem of race differences.

By inviting a group of experts to come together to discuss the racial problem, Unesco was taking up again, after 15 years, a project that the International Institute of Intellectual Co-operation had intended, but had been unable, to carry out.

The scientists who met at Unesco House from 12 to 14 December 1949 were of different nationalities (Brazil, France, India, Mexico, New Zealand, United Kingdom, United States of America). They represented different disciplines; their tendencies were divergent. As the study of man is pursued both in the natural and the social sciences, specialists in both fields are required for a thorough discussion of the racial problem. The scanty representation of the biological sciences on the committee must be attributed to the sudden death of Dr. Ramos and to last-minute withdrawals. The sociologists, who formed the majority of the members, agreed, however, that race had to be defined biologically. The declaration drawn up by this group was published by Unesco on 18 July 1950 and was extremely well received by the general public. It was printed in a considerable number of newspapers in over 18 countries and has frequently been quoted in works dealing with the race problem; the Assembly of the French Union, at its meeting on 20 November 1951, adopted a proposal for the publicizing of the Statement and its inclusion in school syllabuses in the French Union.

It would have been much too optimistic to hope that, in a sphere in which there are so many conflicting trends and methods, the Statement could be considered perfect as it stood. Some of its contentions, and some of the terms used, were much criticized, especially by physical anthropologists and geneticists.

The scientific journal *Man*, published by the Royal Anthropological Institute, and those who criticized this first Statement, did not reject its general spirit nor its main conclusions; they felt it would have been better, however, had certain propositions been put forward with greater circumspection. They considered that the document tended to confuse race as a biological fact and the concept of race as a social phenomenon; they also declined to acknowledge as a proved fact that there are no mental differences between racial groups, stressed that there was insufficient evidence to support that view, and urged the need for keeping an open mind on the subject. The statement that "biological studies lend support to the ethic of universal brotherhood, for man is born with drives towards co-operation" came in for the most frequent criticism.

Some people, not understanding the real significance of the criticisms and comments made on the Statement, tended to regard them as representing a victory for racism and the defeat of a naive humanitarianism. In order to clear up any possible misunderstanding, it was therefore necessary for a second group of scientists, consisting solely, on this occasion, of physical anthropologists and geneticists, chosen, for preference, from among those who had expressed disagreement with the Statement, to draw up a text reflecting more accurately the views of scientific circles. Unesco therefore called on 12 scientists, representing physical anthropology and human genetics, who, in the course of discussions lasting from 4 to 9 June 1951, prepared the document contained in this pamphlet. Generally speaking, the main conclusions of the first Statement were upheld, but some assertions have been toned down and substantial omissions have been made.

It was important to avoid presenting the new Statement as an authoritative manifesto published by Unesco as the last word on the race question. Although the writers of this document sought to make available the results of the most recent research on the question, it was obvious that they could not make full allowance for the doubts still felt by many of their colleagues. Unesco wished to set forth a document expressing not only the opinions of one group of specialists, but also those of other scientists whom it had been impossible to invite to the meeting held in June 1951. For this reason, it was agreed that the Statement should be submitted to as many anthropologists and geneticists as possible, with a request for them to let us have their comments and criticisms before the definitive text was established.[1]

A list of the anthropologists and geneticists consulted appears on page 92. Most of them, after detailed study of the document submitted to them, communicated to us their doubts and objections concerning points of detail, and their views with regard to several more general problems arising out of the Statement.

The number of letters received, the variety and importance of their matter, and the keenness of the discussion, leave no doubt of the interest aroused by this document or of the topicality of the question. The

---

[1] Immediately after the committee's meeting, a number of its members spontaneously suggested amendments and corrections to the text they had all helped to draft. In point of fact, the circumstances in which documents of this type are drawn up are the root cause of the very criticisms which their authors themselves are often the first to formulate. Whole sentences and paragraphs are, in many cases, the result of compromises arrived at in haste. Stylistic details are necessarily neglected when the discussions are primarily concerned with questions of substance. It is therefore very seldom that a document of this length stands in final form at the end of a conference. The improvements in style suggested by the members of the committee were accepted immediately when they were clearly necessary, and after consultation with other members when there was any risk that the substance of the document might be affected by a change of wording.

8

concept of race and the question whether or not there are mental differences between race are highly controversial matters on which anthropologists and geneticists hold widely divergent views, defending them more passionately than any other theory. By printing, with the text of the Statement, all the comments to which it has given rise, Unesco hopes to enable the general public to appreciate the fluctuations of scientific thought on the problem of race. All the scientists who have given us their help have endeavoured to find terms and expressions describing as clearly as possible their understanding of the phenomena with which their own researches are specially concerned. The expressions of approval, impatience and even indignation, and the scruples so often shown in this correspondence about the choice of a word or the order of a paragraph, are not indicative of a more or less frivolous tendency to indulge in verbal quibbles, but represent the exercise of a vital function of science, a basic condition of which is "the proper use of words". A short phrase may often be the outcome of years of research or may epitomize a whole system of thought. The currents and eddies of contemporary scientific development are thus reflected in these hesitations and contradictions. Genetics has revolutionized anthropology and these two branches of study are now seeking a way of fusing into a new integrated whole. The Statement published here, and the comments to which it has given rise, reflect this stage, so rich in possibilities for advances in our knowledge of man.

The replies we have received may be divided into two groups—those evaluating the Statement as a whole and those containing criticisms of detail. A few scientists have put forward their criticisms in the form of a new Statement, free of the defects which, in their opinion, mar the document drawn up by the Unesco committee.

For convenience and clarity, we shall quote extracts from the general letters in one chapter and reserve the detailed criticisms of the Statement for a second chapter; the other draft statements proposed will be contained in a third chapter.

The opinions we quote hereafter have not been polished; they have been written down as the thoughts came into the writer's head; they have the advantage, however, of showing us the current development of concepts now in process of crystallization in scientific theories, which, in turn, will be modified as the sum of our knowledge increases. Those who seek a simple explanation of the differences observed between cultures in biological characteristics will realize that neither the evidence nor "common sense" is on their side. Perhaps they may learn caution from reading this pamphlet. It introduces us to a scientific laboratory and, if confusion seems to be rife, we must not forget that it is precisely such differences of opinion and, indeed, such bitter attacks which give birth to what we call truth.

STATEMENT ON THE NATURE OF RACE AND RACE DIFFERENCES
by Physical Anthropologists and Geneticists—June 1951

1. Scientists are generally agreed that all men living today belong to a single species, *Homo sapiens*, and are derived from a common stock, even though there is some dispute as to when and how different human groups diverged from this common stock.

The concept of race is unanimously regarded by anthropologists as a classificatory device providing a zoological frame within which the various groups of mankind may be arranged and by means of which studies of evolutionary processes can be facilitated. In its anthropological sense, the word "race" should be reserved for groups of mankind possessing well-developed and primarily heritable physical differences from other groups. Many populations can be so classified but, because of the complexity of human history, there are also many populations which cannot easily be fitted into a racial classification.

2. Some of the physical differences between human groups are due to differences in hereditary constitution and some to differences in the environments in which they have been brought up. In most cases, both influences have been at work. The science of genetics suggests that the hereditary differences among populations of a single species are the results of the action of two sets of processes. On the one hand, the genetic composition of isolated populations is constantly but gradually being altered by natural selection and by occasional changes (mutations) in the material particles (genes) which control heredity. Populations are also affected by fortuitous changes in gene frequency and by marriage customs. On the other hand, crossing is constantly breaking down the differentiations so set up. The new mixed populations, in so far as they, in turn, become isolated, are subject to the same processes, and these may lead to further changes. Existing races are

11

merely the result, considered at a particular moment in time, of the total effect of such processes on the human species. The hereditary characters to be used in the classification of human groups, the limits of their variation within these groups, and thus the extent of the classificatory subdivisions adopted may legitimately differ according to the scientific purpose in view.

3. National, religious, geographical, linguistic and cultural groups do not necessarily coincide with racial groups; and the cultural traits of such groups have no demonstrated connexion with racial traits. Americans are not a race, nor are Frenchmen, nor Germans; nor *ipso facto* is any other national group. Muslims and Jews are no more races than are Roman Catholics and Protestants; nor are people who live in Iceland or Britain or India, or who speak English or any other language, or who are culturally Turkish or Chinese and the like, thereby describable as races. The use of the term "race" in speaking of such groups may be a serious error, but it is one which is habitually committed.

4. Human races can be, and have been, classified in different ways by different anthropologists. Most of them agree in classifying the greater part of existing mankind into at least three large units, which may be called major groups (in French *grand-races*, in German *Hauptrassen*). Such a classification does not depend on any single physical character, nor does, for example, skin colour by itself necessarily distinguish one major group from another. Furthermore, so far as it has been possible to analyse them, the differences in physical structure which distinguish one major group from another give no support to popular notions of any general "superiority" or "inferiority" which are sometimes implied in referring to these groups.

Broadly speaking, individuals belonging to different major groups of mankind are distinguishable by virtue of their physical characters, but individual members, or small groups, belonging to different races within the same major group are usually not so distinguishable. Even the major groups grade into each other, and the physical traits by which they and the races within them are characterized overlap considerably. With respect to

12

most, if not all, measurable characters, the differences among individuals belonging to the same race are greater than the differences that occur between the observed averages for two or more races within the same major group.

5. Most anthropologists do not include mental characteristics in their classification of human races. Studies within a single race have shown that both innate capacity and environmental opportunity determine the results of tests of intelligence and temperament, though their relative importance is disputed.

When intelligence tests, even non-verbal, are made on a group of non-literate people, their scores are usually lower than those of more civilized people. It has been recorded that different groups of the same race occupying similarly high levels of civilization may yield considerable differences in intelligence tests. When, however, the two groups have been brought up from childhood in similar environments, the differences are usually very slight. Moreover, there is good evidence that, given similar opportunities, the average performance (that is to say, the performance of the individual who is representative because he is surpassed by as many as he surpasses), and the variation round it, do not differ appreciably from one race to another.

Even those psychologists who claim to have found the greatest differences in intelligence between groups of different racial origin, and have contended that they are hereditary, always report that some members of the group of inferior performance surpass not merely the lowest ranking member of the superior group, but also the average of its members. In any case, it has never been possible to separate members of two groups on the basis of mental capacity, as they can often be separated on a basis of religion, skin colour, hair form or language. It is possible, though not proved, that some types of innate capacity for intellectual and emotional responses are commoner in one human group than in another, but it is certain that, within a single group, innate capacities vary as much as, if not more than, they do between different groups.

The study of the heredity of psychological characteristics is beset with difficulties. We know that certain

13

mental diseases and defects are transmitted from one generation to the next, but we are less familiar with the part played by heredity in the mental life of normal individuals. The normal individual, irrespective of race, is essentially educable. It follows that his intellectual and moral life is largely conditioned by his training and by his physical and social environment.

It often happens that a national group may appear to be characterized by particular psychological attributes. The superficial view would be that this is due to race. Scientifically, however, we realize that any common psychological attribute is more likely to be due to a common historical and social background, and that such attributes may obscure the fact that, within different populations consisting of many human types, one will find approximately the same range of temperament and intelligence.

6. The scientific material available to us at present does not justify the conclusion that inherited genetic differences are a major factor in producing the differences between the cultures and cultural achievements of different peoples or groups. It does indicate, on the contrary, that a major factor in explaining such differences is the cultural experience which each group has undergone.

7. There is no evidence for the existence of so-called "pure" races. Skeletal remains provide the basis of our limited knowledge about earlier races. In regard to race mixture, the evidence points to the fact that human hybridization has been going on for an indefinite but considerable time. Indeed, one of the processes of race formation and race extinction or absorption is by means of hybridization between races. As there is no reliable evidence that disadvantageous effects are produced thereby, no biological justification exists for prohibiting intermarriage between persons of different races.

8. We now have to consider the bearing of these statements on the problem of human equality. We wish to emphasize that equality of opportunity and equality in law in no way depend, as ethical principles, upon the assertion that human beings are in fact equal in endowment.

14

9. We have thought it worth while to set out in a formal manner what is at present scientifically established concerning individual and group differences.

(a) In matters of race, the only characteristics which anthropologists have so far been able to use effectively as a basis for classification are physical (anatomical and physiological).

(b) Available scientific knowledge provides no basis for believing that the groups of mankind differ in their innate capacity for intellectual and emotional development.

(c) Some biological differences between human beings within a single race may be as great as, or greater than, the same biological differences between races.

this only

(d) Vast social changes have occurred that have not been connected in any way with changes in racial type. Historical and sociological studies thus support the view that genetic differences are of little significance in determining the social and cultural differences between different groups of men.

(e) There is no evidence that race mixture produces disadvantageous results from a biological point of view. The social results of race mixture, whether for good or ill, can generally be traced to social factors.

(Text drafted, at Unesco House, Paris, on 8 June 1951, by: Professor R. A. M. Bergman, Royal Tropical Institute, Amsterdam; Professor Gunnar Dahlberg, Director, State Institute for Human Genetics and Race Biology, University of Uppsala; Professor L. C. Dunn, Department of Zoology, Columbia University, New York; Professor J. B. S. Haldane, Head, Department of Biometry, University College, London; Professor M.F. Ashley Montagu, Chairman, Department of Anthropology, Rutgers University, New Brunswick, N.J.; Dr. A. E. Mourant, Director, Blood Group Reference Laboratory, Lister Institute, London; Professor Hans Nachtscheim, Director, Institut für Genetik, Freie Universität, Berlin; Dr. Eugène Schreider, Directeur adjoint du Laboratoire d'Anthropologie Physique de l'Ecole des Hautes Etudes, Paris; Professor Harry L. Shapiro, Chairman, Department of Anthropology, American Museum of Natural History, New York; Dr. J. C. Trevor, Faculty of Archaeology and

Anthropology, University of Cambridge; Dr. Henri V. Vallois, Professeur au Museum d'Histoire Naturelle, Directeur du Musee de l'Homme, Paris; Professor S. Zuckerman, Head, Department of Anatomy, Medical School, University of Birmingham; Professor Th. Dobzhansky, Department of Zoology, Columbia University, New York, and Dr. Julian Huxley contributed to the final wording.)

OBSERVATIONS AND COMMENTS
ON THE STATEMENT AS A WHOLE

The "Statement on the nature of race and race differences" was unreservedly approved by Ackerknecht, Beltrán, Castle, Chattopadhyay, Comas, Connoly, Eickstedt, Grüneberg, Gusinde, Heidelberger, Iltis, Kemp, Komai, Mohr, Park, Reed, Sauter, Sax, Schultz, Skerjl, Snyder, Steinberg, and Steinman.

More scientists, while agreeing with the general tenor of the Statement, made certain criticisms of detail or expressed reservations, some of which affect important points. These scientists include Beaglehole, Birch, Birdsell, Brito da Cunha, Buzzati-Traverso, Clarke, Dreyfus, Frankel, Frota-Pessoa, Herskovits, Howells, Kabir, Landauer, Le Gros Clark, Lipschutz, Luria, Mather, Mayr, Mirsky, Morant, Muller, Needham, Neel, Newman, Penrose, Stern, Stewart, Miss Tildesley, Washburn. Their comments and observations are set forth in the following chapter.

The difficulty of drafting a joint statement, especially in the present state of biological knowledge, did not escape our correspondents. Some of the letters indicate the importance of publishing such a document at the present time. Steinberg, for instance, writes: "Please accept my congratulations on and hearty endorsement of your efforts to place before scientists and the public an accurate picture of the present state of the race question as seen from the point of view of the biologist. Such information has been necessary for years, and of course many excellent attempts have been made in the past to accomplish this; however, as we know, none has been adequately successful. Today, with the growing consciousness of self among the peoples in the less developed areas of the world and among the minority groups in the more advanced nations, it is perhaps more essential than ever that all of us understand the meaning of the observable biological differences among the peoples of the world."

Mayr also hopes that "the authoritative Statement prepared by Unesco will help to eliminate the pseudo-scientific race conceptions which have been used as excuses for many injustices and even shocking crimes". "I applaud and wholeheartedly endorse [it]," he writes, adding: "It cannot be emphasized too strongly that all so-called races are variable populations, and that there is often more difference between extreme individuals of one race than between certain individuals of different races. All human races are mixtures of populations and the term "pure race" is an absurdity. The second important point which needs stressing is that genetics plays a very minor part in the cultural characteristics of different peoples.... The third point is that equality of opportunity and equality in law do not depend on physical, intellectual and genetic identity. There are striking differences in physical, intellectual and other genetically founded qualities among individuals of even the most homogeneous human population, even among brothers and sisters. No acknowledged ethical principle exists which would permit denial of equal opportunity for reason of such differences to any member of the human species."

Mirsky likewise stresses the timeliness of this Statement. "The value of the present statement is clearly seen when one reads such a thing as the recent article by C. D. Darlington published by Unesco (*International Social Science Bulletin*, Vol. II, 1950, p. 479). In this article, entitled 'The Genetic Understanding of Race in Man', the reader who is not well versed in genetics and is not acquainted with Darlington might be led to suppose that certain ideas on race followed quite reasonably from an application of the accepted principles of mendelism to human populations. If the reader of Darlington's article had also read the Unesco Statement on Race it would be obvious to him that the 'understanding of race' expounded in that article is derived not from the principles of genetics but from the guesses and prejudices of Darlington.

"The Unesco Statement on Race signed by a group of distinguished geneticists should help the reader who encounters uncritical writings on race purporting to be based on the principles of genetics."

Park finds the Statement "authoritative, disinterested

and non-propagandist" and congratulates the committee "on such a cogent presentation".

Comas, who signed the first Statement assures us of his agreement with the substance and the text of the second: "As an anthropologist and a member of the committee that drafted the 1950 Statement, I wish publicly to express my full agreement with the Statement on Race drawn up by Unesco in 1951 with the help of some of the most eminent among anthropologists and geneticists, men whose names are a guarantee of objectivity and scientific integrity."

The race question raises the problem of the relations between science and ethics. On this point Landauer disagrees with the authors of the Statement: " I am in whole-hearted sympathy, of course, with the intentions of the framers of this manifesto, but I fear that my philosophy differs in one basic point. I *do* believe that the results of scientific investigations can greatly strengthen ethical judgments arrived at in some other fashion. I do *not* believe that ethical values can ever be directly derived from scientific data. It is always the analytic mind which approaches the data in one way or another. It seems to me that the Unesco document was written on the assumption that from a certain body of scientific facts *necessarily* flowed certain ethical commandments. Perhaps because of this there was, I feel, some yielding to the temptation to treat *terra incognita* as *terra nullius*. It would surely make no difference to the ethical standards of the Unesco group or to mine if, for instance, an unequal distribution of genes for certain mental traits were demonstrated. The declaration that 'all men are created equal was a fine one and remains so, even though and in the best sense *because* it is untrue in the biological sphere.

"I hope that I have made myself clear. If not, I will gladly try again. But, possibly apart from minor specific suggestions, and in spite of some mental reservations, I would rather see the manifesto given out than nothing to happen."

Altogether, the terminology and some of the phrasing of the Statement have been thought to be too technical or not clear enough for the lay public to whom it is addressed. Stewart particularly emphasizes this twofold shortcoming: "I feel that the committee which formu-

19

lated this Statement, like the first committee, was thinking more about its colleagues than about laymen. Scientists do not need a statement on race; laymen need a statement written in language that they can understand. Why should the simplification of the Statement on Race be left to newspaper writers? Why not have Unesco's own Statement in a form simple enough for anyone to understand? Take, for example, the first paragraph of your new statement: It is not about race at all, and does not tie in with the succeeding paragraph. This first paragraph is about species and 'common stock', these are technical terms and are not explained. I could go on and cite other examples of the use of terminology meaningful only to the professional." And Stewart, to illustrate what he means by a Statement on Race that everyone can understand, sent us the text of a statement which will be found further on (see pp. 78-79).

Newman, while agreeing with the substance of the text, criticizes the faults of scientific style and presentation: "On the matter of organization," he writes, "it is my opinion that the Statement lacks a good flow of ideas. It could and should be written so that each of the eight points leads in a logical manner to the next one, that the weight of the reasoning becomes greater as the reader proceeds. As the Statement stands, it is choppy and disconnected as though fabricated by patchwork. One way out lies in the fact that there are two closely allied sets of points: 1, 4, 7, and 3, 6. Thus a more cogent organization could be achieved by the following order of points: 1, 7, 4, 2, 5, 3, 6. The first three deal with what race is, race mixture and race classification. Item 2 explains how races are formed. Then item 5 covers the denial of racial differences in intellectual capacity. The last two items tell us what race is not. The order gives a fair flow, especially if interconnecting sentences are used to lead from one item to the next."

Steinberg also proposes to invert the order of points 3 and 4, and he adds: "Finally, may I suggest that the release for the general public be prepared by an experienced popularizer of science, such as Amran Scheinfeld, author of *You and Heredity* and *Women and Men?* I have submitted the Statement to some physicians and to some others who, while college graduates with advanced degrees, are not trained in science, and all of them have

found the Statement very difficult to read and to some
extent completely obscure. Sectons 1, 2 and 4 do, after
all, presume a fair amount of familiarity with genetics."

Mirsky finds the Statement "far longer and more
involved than need be. The present biological point of
view on race, if stated without regard to the attitude of
those biologists who have themselves been influenced by
race prejudice, could be far simpler and more concise".

Beltrán feels strongly that the document would be
considerably more useful if Section 2 contained a few
explanatory sentences to make it more intelligible to the
uninitiated. "Even in its present form, however," he
writes, "I think it is an accurate statement, based on
scientific data, and extremely helpful in clarifying the
dangerous problem of human races, particularly in view
of the great authority conferred upon it by the prestige
of its signatories...."

In the opinion of some geneticists, the only fault in
the Statement is that it is not full enough and leaves
out of account one or more important aspects of the race
question. This was the view, in particular, of Mr. Dreyfus, who wrote us the following letter shortly before his
death: "I agree, in principle, with the terms of the
Statement. There are, however, several questions calling
for comment. The most important requirement has
been fulfilled, as the Statement is signed by persons of
great prestige in widely different fields. It was obviously
necessary to avoid making the Statement too broad.
Apart from these two points, I think the major criticisms
to be made are, firstly, that the genetic substratum of
certain characteristics has not been brought out sufficiently clearly. This is the case with regard to musical
talent, which, admittedly, can develop only in a suitable
environment, but which is quite obviously of genetic
origin. It is clear that efforts have been made to exclude
from the Statement anything which might justify racial
discrimination; but this very proper concern should not
be allowed to take precedence over scientific truth. It is
only necessary to quote the case of Mozart. Secondly, a
question which, in my view, deserves more attention is
that of emphasizing the difference between animal
strains and human races. Among the latter (and in artificially selected races) we find problems unknown in
animal strains, such, for example, as polymorphism

21

(which is found only occasionally and on a very small scale in certain natural strains, such as *Drosophila polymorpha*). It would, I think, be useful to show that, among the human races, somatic characteristics were probably originally selected according to natural fitness, but, as a result of the development of civilization, characteristics which were once adaptive have been superseded at the present time, therefore, selection is of very minor importance, because civilization has given man the means of overcoming natural conditions. In other words, while in the early days of the human races, it was a good thing to have a white skin in cold climates and a black in hot climates, civilization has now placed within our reach a whole series of expedients whereby the white man can protect himself against the discomforts of a hot climate and the black man against those of a cold climate, so that the initial advantage is, for all practical purposes, cancelled, out. It is for this precise reason that the races, and especially those most directly in touch with civilization, have become so varied and therefore so difficult to define.

"Thirdly, it would be well to point out that, so far as somatic characteristics, are concerned, man is mainly the product of heredity, while, from the point of view of his mental characteristics, he is rather a product of environment (cf. experiments with identical twins brought up in different conditions, and tests quoted by Klineberg in his pamphlet published by Unesco)."

Brito da Cunha in his letter mentions certain points he would have liked to be developed in the Statement: "I read it [the Statement] carefully and I think it is very fine. However, I think that there is one point that should be considered.... In the early days of mankind natural selection certainly had a very important role in the differentiation of populations. Physical characters were selected in different regions according to the ecological factors dominant in the habitat. Physical characters such as skin pigmentation, body build, etc. (see *Races*, by Coon, Garn and Birdsell), had different adaptive values in relation to the geographical distribution of man. Human races were produced mainly by an adaptive response to the ecology of the habitat and their formation was directed by natural selection accompanied by genetic drift in small populations For these

22

reasons in the early days of man it was possible to speak in terms of superior or inferior races relative to a specific habitat. In tropical regions the Negro race was probably superior to the white because it was adapted to the tropical environment and the white race was not. The white race had the similar adaptive superiority to the Negro in temperate regions, etc.

"With the progress of civilization these physical characters became less and less important. Today these characters are protected from the effects of natural selection by the techniques introduced by civilization. The adaptive physical characters that differentiate human races are today completely unimportant. The adaptive values of various physical characters in which human races differ is probably nearly the same in modern life. However, they were important enough in the early days of man to be affected by natural selection.

"In regard to intellectual qualities, higher intelligence was adaptive everywhere, all the time. Natural selection selected for higher intelligence in all human populations and for that reason human races do not differ in intellectual qualities.

"I think that it is very important to show in the Statement the difference in importance of the physical characters in primitive and civilized populations. The physical characters that differentiate human races *were* certainly important in primitive populations but they are today negligible.

"On the other hand, intellectual qualities have always been the object of ortho-selection in all populations, and for this reason human races do not differ in regard to them.

"If some day the physical characters that differentiate races are studied physiologically, differences which can be related to the ecology of the habitat will certainly be found. This point can be taken by racists to make dangerous speculations. That is the reason why I think it is important to consider these points in the Unesco Statement."

Mohr gives the Statement his full assent, but makes one comment which deserves to be quoted *in extenso:* "Many of the present misconceptions about 'race' are due to the fact that people are used to the term 'race' in domesticated animals, and accordingly are inclined to

23

transfer their associations from races in domesticated animals to human material. It might therefore eventually be useful to explain the fallacy of this procedure by emphasizing the fact that 'races' in domesticated animals are the result of inbreeding and artificial selection for special hereditary traits, a situation that is fundamentally different from that prevailing in human propagation. So much confusion is due to the fact that one and the same term is used with different meanings.

"The above does not apply to the English language, which has the term 'breed' when it is a question of domesticated animals. But in other languages, including the Nordic languages, the same word 'race' is used in both fields, thus creating much confusion."

Penrose too believes that "use of the term 'race' must be discontinued altogether. Much of the 'statement' could thus be automatically rendered unnecessary and the rest of it could be strengthened and made clearer.

"The concept of the races of man is inexact and archaic. It belongs to an unscientific epoch and it cannot be used without perpetuating confusion and engendering discord. The objects of study in scientific anthropology are collections of people or *populations*. These can be precisely defined geographically, genealogically, linguistically or culturally according to the needs of any particular investigation which is to be carried out. The frequency of a given measurement or of a given character trait, physical or behaviouristic, can be objectively determined in any given population. The question of the genetical or environmental significance of the character can be discussed independently, provided that reference to the old concept of racial grouping is avoided because of its latent implication that racial characters are inherited....

"If the terms 'race' and 'racial groups' are dropped from the scientific vocabulary, the points made in Section 3 are covered by saying that all statements using such terms are untrustworthy. The discussion in Section 4 seems confused because no indication is given about how the populations classified as 'major groups' are defined.

"On the positive side, I welcome wholeheartedly most of the ideas put forward in Sections 5, 6, 7, especially the last paragraph of Section 5....

"At present there is no evidence that man can be divided biologically into subspecies as, indeed, is stated in the first sentence of Section 1. Unless and until such evidence is forthcoming, the term 'race' has only one rational use in anthropology, namely to apply to the whole human race as distinct from other species.

"I think that the interests which Unesco has in mind in publishing this Statement could best be served by frankly admitting that the concept of the existence of different human racial groups is obsolete and superfluous in scientific enquiry. Support for the use of the mystical term 'race' in this connexion by scientists is likely to encourage superstition and prejudice in popular discussions. Clear thinking, which is the best antidote to prejudice, can be aided by referring only to human populations; these are real and they can be precisely defined.

Mather's comments turn upon the conception of "race" and the terminology and spirit of the Statement. This is what he says:

"As with all biological classification, the tendency is to use the notion of 'race' in men as one level in a hierarchical classification. I need not mention the difficulties which systematists have often found with such classification. They will always arise when relations are reticulate. The mixing and crossing that has gone on, and is now going on, in man will thus inevitably make difficulties for such a classification. One can perhaps still use the notion of race in a statistical sense, but the extent and value of its use then becomes a problem requiring investigation in its own right.

"Race is essentially a genetical idea, implying community of descent within the race and some corresponding (though not necessarily complete) measure of isolation between races. The difficulties raised by incomplete isolation have been mentioned; but whatever the position in this respect, there must always remain the problem of how to detect and gauge genetical differences. It must be done by observation of the phenotype without, in man, the aid of controlled breeding experiments. No one phenotypic character can have the monopoly of giving information. We must be prepared to use whatever characters are available and useful. Indeed the more characters that are examined, the more information we are likely to obtain. Thus different characters may give different information, in that each is but an imperfect guide to the genetic situation, so that each anthropologist may be led to define race in his own peculiar way.

"The terminology of the draft statement seemed to me to be loose, even to the point of ambiguity in places. I believe that rewording would be well worthwhile if the document is to stand up to criticism.

"The aim of the document was not always clear to me, perhaps in part because of the somewhat loose terminology and partly, I suspect, because of its political implications. I felt that at times it was bending over backwards to deny the existence of race in the sense that this term has been used for political purposes in the recent past. *I, of course, entirely agree in condemning Nazi race theory, but I do not think that the case against it is strengthened by playing down the possibility of statistical differences in, for example, the mental capacities of different human groups.* They *may not* be there, though this would surprise me, but the fact that we have at present no evidence does not mean that they *are not* there. The important point, politically, is surely that the group differences are only statistical; that there is immense overlap of individuals from different groups; that there is no 'pure' race with an unconditional superiority of all its individuals over others. The case for this view (and hence for the proper treatment of, and giving of adequate opportunity to, all peoples) does not rest on the absence of average differences, and, it seems to me, is not strengthened by denying the possibility of such differences."

Darlington, Fisher, Genna and Coon are frankly opposed to the Statement.

Darlington's judgment of the whole document is as follows:

"The proposal to issue an agreed statement on race 'entirely satisfactory' to both anthropologists and geneticists was likely to lead to a result partly meaningless and partly negative. In addition however this statement is partly untrue and capable of being contradicted at once.... Summing up. There is a danger that any statement about race issued by people who disagree with the Nazi views on race expressed 20 years ago by Hitler,

26

Rosenberg and Streicher will be designed as a reply to those views. Since the Nazi views were emotional in expression and political in purpose, any discussion of them by scientists should be explicit, and explicitly separate from the expression of scientific opinions. Otherwise their opinions will be confused by the emotional and political issues.

"This confusion is found throughout the first Unesco Statement on Race and in all the last six paragraphs of the second Statement.

"Today we understand very much more about how human society has evolved than Darwin did; but few of us know the results of this evolution by our own observations better than he did. Fortunately genetics has given us every reason to agree with him. In *The Descent of Man* he writes: 'The races differ also in constitution, in acclimatization, and in liability to certain diseases. Their mental characteristics are likewise very distinct; chiefly as it would appear in their emotional, but partly in their intellectual faculties.'

"By trying to prove that races do not differ in these respects we do no service to mankind. We conceal the greatest problem which confronts mankind (and particularly in respect of the organization of Unesco) namely how to use the diverse, the ineradicably diverse, gifts, talents, capacities of each race for the benefit of all races. For if we were all innately the same how should it profit us to work together? And what an empty world it would be."

Sir Ronald Fisher has one fundamental objection to the Statement, which, as he himself says, destroys the very spirit of the whole document. He believes that human groups differ profoundly "in their innate capacity for intellectual and emotional development" and concludes from this that the "practical international problem is that of learning to share the resources of this planet amicably with persons of materially different nature, and that this problem is being obscured by entirely well intentioned efforts to minimize the real differences that exist".

Genna writes: "What is set forth in the Statement on Race undoubtedly corresponds to the present stage of scientific knowledge about race regarded biologically. It may however be doubted whether such statements

27

are of any use at all in the combating of race prejudice.

"It should also be observed that in order to oppose race prejudice there would not seem to be any need to prove that human races are equal as regards psychical attributes.... Prejudice should be combated even if the psychical qualities of races differed very greatly. Knowledge of the psychological differences between human races is at present fluid and it would seem impossible to deny altogther the existence of these differences—at any rate as regards certain psychological aptitudes of the major groups—unless we are prepared to admit that these differences imply a racial hierarchy. In the absence of more exact information, it does not seem right to regard the problem as settled by a mere negative.

"These considerations are particularly inspired by the five points in the Report's conclusions; these are not convincing."

Coon's general impression is as follows:

"The spirit is fine, it is wholly in keeping with the trends of the times, as Toynbee pointed out in the *New York Times* (Magazine section, 21 October 1951). This, said Toynbee, is not the Atomic Age, but the Age of Human Equality, or some such words. In other words, for the first time we are beginning to realize the unity and importance of human beings and the need for giving everyone an equal chance. Of that I approve 100 per cent.

"However, *I do not* approve of slanting scientific data to support a social theory, since that is just what the Russians are doing, and what Hitler did. If we are right, the facts will bear us out. I think they do. The corrections I have suggested are made with that in view.

"I hope that you don't mind my frankness. This is too important a matter for punch-pulling. The essence of my criticisms are that we should be positive or say we don't know; that we should not rely on negative evidence."

Summers does not conceal his disappointment at the Statement:

"The need for a statement on race by a committee of anthropologists of unimpeachable international repute is great. For a person such as myself whose home and family are situated in a heterogeneous community such statements have a practical value (for good or evil) which is hardly realized by those of my colleagues who live in homogeneous communities and in academic environments.

"There is little doubt in my mind that, in Southern and Central Africa at any rate, relations between white and black are becoming more strained. There is a dangerous current of emotionalism starting to run and anything that scientists can do to present an objective picture of the meaning of race is desirable.

"It is with these thoughts in my mind that I have read and reread your draft statement. Unfortunately, I cannot compliment my colleagues on the result of their labours for the draft statement fails lamentably in the primary purpose of objective presentation referred to above.

"To come to details:

"The Statement is in obscure language and in places it is not expressed in good English—it reads like a third-rate translation from German (Sections 3, 5 and 8 are especially bad).

"It is in places illogical (the worst example is the attempt to explain a statistical investigation given in the centre of page 3. Section 7 is equally unsound in logic, since negative evidence is no justification for the conclusion.

"Finally, the whole Statement smacks of special pleading and cannot possibly appeal either to educated non-anthropologists because of its poorness of expression, nor can it appeal to hard-headed businessmen—whether capitalists or trades unionists—because its lack of logic will be at once evident.

"I therefore beg of my colleagues to address themselves once more to this extremely difficult but important task. Such a statement must be in clear language, unambiguous and without attempts to explain unimportant points, it also must be without obvious political bias and must be entirely objective (even to the extent of dropping pet theories which an anthropologist can detect peeping out here and there).

"Should anyone wish to take any notice of my remarks I ought to add that in this self-governing Colony in which I settled some four or five years ago after living for many years in England, I am regarded as distinctly pro-Native, nevertheless I cannot feel that the draft

Statement is going to help me in the least in my very difficult struggle for improved race relations. I shall, by virtue of my anthropological knowledge, be expected to interpret your Statement to my fellow citizens, black and white: as it stands this task is an impossible one because I cannot understand my distinguished colleagues' point of view which seems to possess all the disadvantages of a hastily contrived compromise."

Although he says that "The Unesco Statement on Race, 1951, contains many conclusions which are strongly supported by scientific knowledge, and perhaps none which can be rigorously proven to be incorrect", Stern has nevertheless the impression "that it is somewhat coloured by its good intentions". He ends his letter with the following considerations: "If Science wants to destroy prejudice it can only hope to accomplish this if its position is as relatively unassailable as its very best founded facts. Our knowledge of the importance of genetic and non-genetic factors in accounting for group differences in mankind has not yet reached that position. To believe and to make popular use of the belief that a decision has been obtained, or nearly obtained, may well make it more difficult to attain the goal of enlightenment. At present the prestige of science can often be used to support the clear and strong statement: 'It is not proven,' but it seems to me doubtful whether it can be used effectively by opposing fatally wrong ideas with opinions which still remain subject to discussion."

Through Nachtsheim, the text of the Statement was shown to a number of German anthropologists and geneticists. We received replies from Fischer, Lenz, Saller, Scheidt and Weinert.

Lenz gathers that Unesco's only purpose in holding these two meetings of experts was to combat anti-Semitism. Obviously, however, anti-Semitism is only one aspect of racism and Unesco has made no distinction between the different forms of it. The same charge is made in Walter Scheidt's letter.

Lenz criticizes the Statement in these words: "In my opinion one of the dangers of the present Statement is that it disregards not only the enormous hereditary differences between men, but also absence of selection as the decisive cause of the decline of civilization, and it therefore runs counter to the science of eugenics. I presume that this is not Unesco's intention.

"The 1949 Statement, which was intended to counteract anti-Semitism, failed in its purpose owing to the unfortunate way in which it was worded, and it gave rise to much criticism; this error should not be repeated.

"In conclusion, I would like to refer to the book written by H. J. Muller, C. C. Little and L. H. Snyder, *Genetics, Medicine and Man* (Cornell University Press, Ithaca, 1947). The authors express the hope that the continued increase in biological knowledge will destroy the fallacious concept of the equality or similarity of all men and the current belief in the omnipotence of social influences. 'In so doing genetics will steadily exert a highly desirable pressure on human thought in the direction of unselfish interest in and attention to coming generations and the future welfare of mankind.' I do not think that anyone will challenge the competence of these three distinguished American biologists. Further, the word 'innate', which is used more than once, also seems rather inappropriate. I presume it is meant to designate what is not determined by environment. In fact, however, many innate characteristics are determined by environment, whereas many hereditary characteristics do not reveal themselves immediately after the birth of the persons in question, but only later. I therefore suggest that the word 'innate' be replaced by the word 'hereditary'."

Fischer, invited, like the scientists named above, to give his views on the Statement, considers it an attempt to impose an anti-scientific doctrine. He writes:

"In so far as the Statement condemns any defamation of races and emphasizes the appalling nature of the recent abuse of racial theory, it has my full and unqualified approval. I wholeheartedly agree, also, with its explicit and implicit finding that anthropology and racial studies afford no justification for the assumption that the members of any particular race are not entitled to the enjoyment of all fundamental rights, or for any form distinguished men as the authors of this Statement. of racial discrimination. And I am very glad that, after all the horrors that have been perpetrated, these principles should have been enunciated clearly and publicized widely by an organization of such standing and by such

"But the Statement also purports to be an authoritative body of scientific doctrines, and this is quite a different matter. Without touching upon the content of these doctrines, and quite apart from whether or not they meet with my approval, I must register my fundamental opposition to the advancing of scientific theses as such, and protest against it.

"I recall the National Socialists' notorious attempts to establish certain doctrines as the only correct conclusions to be drawn from research on race, and their suppression of any contrary opinion; as well as the Soviet Government's similar claim on behalf of Lysenko's theory of heredity, and its condemnation of Mendel's teaching. The present Statement likewise puts forward certain scientific doctrines as the only correct ones, and quite obviously expects them to receive general endorsement as such. I repeat that, without assuming any attitude towards the substance of the doctrines in the Statement, I am opposed to the principle of advancing them as doctrines. The experiences of the past have strengthened my conviction that freedom of scientific enquiry is imperilled when any scientific findings or opinions are elevated, by an authoritative body, into the position of doctrines."

Scheidt regards the Statement as not less tendentious than Nazi publications on race. He writes:

"You must surely be acquainted with my attitude towards Unesco's Statement on Race. It is my belief that, had due heed been paid to the definition I gave of races in 1923 as complexes of in-bred hereditary characteristics, and to my research which helped to demonstrate the methods and difficulties of proving the existence of breeding in man, they would have been equally effective in averting the tragic errors of the National Socialists and the repetition in this Statement of *all* the same errors in reverse.

"But it is, of course, a matter of no importance that I should disagree with this Statement as strongly as I did with the National Socialist ravings about race and with the anthropology that was then the vogue. I can have no part in attempts to solve scientific questions by political manifestoes, as is the practice in Soviet Russia and now at Unesco as well. If, however, I can help you at all in your delicate task of taking account of German

32

scientific opinion in such matters, I am, of course, entirely at your disposal and will ask you for your instructions. But, as you see, I am inclined to think that an objective discussion of these matters is far from being the aim of the group of experts. I also imagine that it would be reluctant to give Germans an opportunity of participating objectively in the discussions. Any objection which Germans might raise to this Statement (which is in flat contradicton with the present policy of nearly all Unesco's Member States) would probably be misconstrued as a survival of Nazi ideas.

"I do not feel that this state of things will impede the progress of scientific research; but I also see no advantage in an objective revision and correction of the Statement. Scientific anthropology has passed through the genetic periods which ended, provisionally, in 1930 and from which, in the current state of research in genetics, general physiology and general psychology, there was no more to hope; it now has far more urgent matters to study, comprised, as I see it, in the old problem of the relationship between body and soul. When once fresh ground has been broken by these investigations and by the necessary research on mutation and heredity, which must be experimental and confined to the fields of zoology and botany if it is to be of any value, it will perhaps be possible to revert to the still unsolved problems of race and biology. In my opinion, this research will probably not be completed within the lifetime of our own generation or the next.

"If therefore the Statement achieves its purpose of condemning, once and for all, research conducted into the cultural and biological aspects of race, the rational development of these studies will not be greatly prejudiced. For an anthropology that now, in these days of political and other kinds of ineptitude, reverts to the pre-genetic theories current at the turn of the century and to the problems of man's origin that occupied nineteenth-century scientific thought, is doomed, whether approved by a manifesto or not. Its official demise is a virtual certainty, thanks to the anthropologists fashionable in the days of nationalism."

Saller also wonders what can be the purpose of the Statement: "It cannot, obviously, be intended as a dogmatic statement designed to settle the racial problem once and for all. Its only purpose can be to give the general public certain facts on the basis of which the public can say that science today takes this or that point of view. All that is contained in such a statement need not, therefore, be uncontroversial. It does seem to me, in this connexion, that this particular Statement very skilfully evades many disputed issues.

"Coming down to more specific details, I feel that there is a certain danger in the Statement, especially in so far as the drafts hitherto evolved have utterly disregarded or even flatly denied the existence of mental (psychic) differences between certain groups of peoples. We may or may not give the name of race to such groups of human beings, who differ in their inherited psychic characteristics; but the whole science of eugenics is based on the existence of such hereditary psychic differences. At one time it was called race hygiene in Germany, its connexion with racial questions thus being emphasized. In view of the work carried out in the field of eugenics, I consider it advisable to formulate these points more carefully in the proposed statement, and in any case to leave more doors open than are left in the present Statement. There is no need to base oneself *ab initio* on such hereditary differences, or to place undue emphasis on their results; but it is essential to admit the possibility both of their existence and of its having certain consequences, as otherwise one may later be forced into a retraction.

"I should like to add a few words on the concept of so-called pure races, which, in my opinion, is self-contradictory; the idea of pure races among human beings should be dropped altogether. Anthropology knows no pure races, as understood by geneticists, since every race of human beings is characterized by a certain variability, a factor which precludes the genetic purity of any race. All these problems should therefore be stated with far greater caution and less categorically. I would advocate drawing a clear distinction between the term 'race' as applied to human beings and the definitions of race used by geneticists, so as to put an end to all talk of pure and mixed races among human beings.

"More might be said in regard to the Statement; but in view of the purpose of the latter, as I have interpreted it above, all that is really important is the

34

criticism which I have confined to the two foregoing points."

Weinert rejects the Statement, in the first place because it contains self-evident facts, and secondly, because two of its points seem to him to be untrue: "I consider nearly all the statements put forward to be self-evident, and doubt the necessity of convening a special conference on the subject. The reason for the Statement was obviouly the Nazi period in Germany. Of course, all men and women are equal as human beings, and none has the right to persecute another on grounds of race, religion or politics. But such persecutions are confined neither to the years 1933-45 nor to Germany alone. They are as old as the ideas which breed them and will probably, despite all statements, continue.

"In my opinion, some of the statements made in Section 3 do not correspond to the facts. Many of the groups mentioned do actually coincide with racial groups. *In regard to Section 7:* Whether there is any biological justification for considering races to differ in value does not alter the fact that human beings themselves attach different values to their races. Consequently, half-castes always try to win recognition as members of a higher race, but this the latter race generally denies them. In defence of prohibiting marriage between persons of different races, I should like to ask which of the gentlemen who signed the Statement would be prepared to marry his daughter for example to an Australian aboriginal. *In regard to Section 9 (b),* if it is true that all races have the same innate capacity for intellectual development, then why is it that so far only the members of the white race have built up any scientific knowledge?

"In my opinion, such statements can never be as effective as a firm determination to persuade civilized peoples to be active in preventing and eradicating all inhumanity, especially in so far as it is liable to arise within their own particular group."

COMMENTS AND CRITICISMS ON DIFFERENT ITEMS IN THE STATEMENT

In this chapter, we reproduce the criticisms made of various assertions contained in the Statement. As the form of the document is so important, we have also included amendments of words or sentences which have been suggested to us.

For the reader's convenience, we reproduce, in each case, the phrase or sentence referred to in the comments. When an amendment proposed by one of our correspondents has, with the agreement of the committee's members, been incorporated in the text, we have not felt it necessary to mention it.

SECTION 1

Lenz subjects this whole section to criticisms which are so fundamental in nature that they deserve to be quoted in full:

"In my opinion, the Linnaen theory that all men belong to a single species is inaccurate. Moreover, it is by no means true that this theory is accepted by scientists in general. In his well-known *Lehrbuch der Anthropologie* (Manual of Physical Anthropology), Rudolf Martin speaks of the 'Sub-groups of the Hominids'; 'Opinions are divided on the question whether these sub-groups are to be regarded as species or simply varieties of species in the zoological sense of the term.' (2nd Ed., Vol. I, Jena, 1928, p. 7.)

"Another distinguished scientist, Erwin Baur, says in his *Einführung in die Vererbungslehre* (Introduction to the Theory of Heredity), 1930, Ed., p. 41: 'If we cross-breed some three or four fundamentally different, but interfertile *Antirrhinum* species (which therefore mendelize) and allow the hybrid offspring to reproduce in millions through complete panmixia, the result will be an *Antirrhinum* community in which further numerous mutations will appear and persist, and this community will be almost as varied as the population of the present Reich.' This comparison seems to me to be an excellent one, but such a hybrid community could not be called a species.

"If an unprejudiced scientist were confronted with a West-African Negro, an Eskimo and a North-West European, he could hardly consider them to belong to the same 'species'. Numerous 'good' species by no means reveal such considerable differences. Only one thing is certain: all men belong to the same genus. The possibility of fertile crossing is not a conclusive criterion of a common stock. Many species of plants and animals produce, through artificial crossbreeding, fertile and readily mendelizing hybrid offspring and are nevertheless true species.

"As far as I am aware, neither African pygmies nor Bushmen interbreed with Negroes or with Europeans; thus, owing to their natural instincts and their habits, they are physiologically isolated. It would no doubt be possible to crossbreed them artificially with other races, but that would be no proof that they belong to a common stock.

"In my opinion, the term *Homo sapiens,* which is used in Section 1, is a misnomer. As is well known, it was invented by Linnaeus, who did not however give any diagnosis or description of his *Homo sapiens.* On the other hand, he gave diagnoses of several human species which he recognized as such *(Hominum species)* and to which he gave binary names. Thus, even from the historical point of view, the term *Homo sapiens* is unjustifiable. It seems to me that the term 'species' cannot be appropriately applied to the whole of mankind, though I will not maintain dogmatically that there are different human species.

"With regard to the term 'race', most anthropologists do not regard it as a purely 'classificatory device', which would lead to an artificial system such as that of Linnaeus. Anthropologists who study racial questions are more interested in establishing genetic subdivisions of the human genus. Since Blumenbach, Kant, Topinard and others, racial differences are deemed to include hereditary differences and not merely 'primarily heritable physical differences'. Differences due to environment are not racial differences."

Scientists are generally agreed that all men belong to a single species, Homo sapiens, and are derived from a common stock, even though there is some dispute as to when and how different human groups diverged from this common stock.

"What does 'and are derived from a common stock' mean?" asks Mather, and he adds: "Presumably that man has a single line of descent and is not a fusion of several lines which diverged for part of the time in his ancestry. Even, however, if man were polyphyletic he would still be derived from a common stock if one went far enough back, so that this phrase is not really informative."

The concept of race is unanimously regarded by anthropologists as a classificatory device providing a zoological frame within which the various groups of mankind may be arranged....

Le Gros Clark does not like this sentence because "the concept of race is not *of itself* (and entirely) a classificatory device, though attempts have been made to use it as such. This sentence should, I think, better read: 'The concept of race has its origin in the recognition of physical differences in certain major groups of mankind, and has been developed by anthropologists as a classificatory device, etc.' "

Nor is Frota-Pessoa satisfied with this definition, for these reasons: "In item 1, second paragraph, the concept of race lacks precision and completeness. To write that 'The concept of race is . . . a classificatory device providing a zoological frame within which the various groups of mankind may be arranged' makes the race concept more artificial than it really is. It is not only a 'classificatory device'; it results chiefly from the recognition of a natural fact, namely, that human populations differ in the incidence and frequence of certain hereditary characters. This is stated later on, but the wording as it stands gives a greater emphasis to the artificial classificatory role of the race concept, instead of emphasizing its importance for the understanding of the actual biological texture of mankind."

38

Needham objects to the use of the word "zoological", which to him suggests inferior creatures. He would prefer either that the adjective be omitted or that it be replaced by "anthropological" or "ethnological".

. . . and by means of which studies of evolutionary processes can be facilitated.

These words do not appear in the original Statement. They were added at the suggestion of Birdsell, who thinks that without them the concept of race is much too restricted and ignores "the more dynamic processes of evolution". Haldane did not favour the insertion of this clause, despite support given to it by several of his colleagues. For this reason: "On the contrary, I think that it is quite probable that this classification may actually make the study of evolutionary processes more difficult, as it is not impossible that different peoples belonging to the same 'race' may have arisen polyphylatically."

Herskovits is also against the inclusion of this particular statement which does not add "anything to the discussion, and suggests a possible implication that there are significant differentials in degree of evolution of different races, something I am sure there is no desire to imply".

In its anthropological sense, the word "race" should be reserved for groups of mankind possessing well-developed and primarily heritable physical differences from other groups.

Frota-Pessoa considers that this is not altogether true at the present stage of scientific research: "It should be interesting to add that, from the genetical point of view, even not 'well-developed' differences suffice for distinguishing races (cf. Dobzhansky [1]): 'Races may be defined as populations which differ in the frequencies of some genes.') This addition is good for the sake of emphasizing that major and minor racial groups differ only in degree, but not qualitatively, and also to destroy the apparent contradiction that this sentence presents with the following statement quoted from the second

---

[1] Theodosius Dobzhansky, "The Genetic Nature of Differences among Men," in *Evolutionary Thought in America*, New Haven, Yale University Press, 1950, p. 99.

paragraph of item 4: '. . . but individual members, or small groups, belonging to different races within the same major group are usually not so distinguishable.' If only 'well-developed' differences were able for distinguishing races, even 'small groups belonging to different races' should be distinguishable."

SECTION 2

Krogman's comment on the whole paragraph was this: "This is well and cogently written at a high level of scientific understanding. I read it to neighbours (college graduates in arts and sciences) and they did not get it. For one thing, it conveys a spurious idea that we really know human genetics. Greatest exception was taken to the last sentence, which implies that the 'scientific purpose in view' may juggle with what are presumed to be basic (genetic) data. This hint of the lability of genetic concepts in human races suggest the possibility of 'bending facts' to fit political (racial) expediency."

Some of the physical differences between human groups are due to differences in hereditary constitution and some to differences in the environments in which they have been brought up.
After objecting to the use of the word "race" in anthropology, Penrose proposed that in point 2 the word "groups" should be replaced by "populations" and that instead of "differences between races" they should say "differences between isolated populations".

In most cases, both influences have been at work (the original version spoke of *"in many cases"*).
This phrase was criticized in almost identical terms by Beaglehole, Kabir, Mather and Needham. The first wrote: "It seems to me that your phrase *'in many cases'* is a very definite understatement of the case. I should have thought that the best phrase to use would have been 'in all cases' since I imagine that it must be extremely difficult to find a human group in which it is possible definitely to say that, of the differences which separate this group from another, some are absolutely and specifically due to hereditary constitution and some

40

absolutely and specifically due to differences in environment." Kabir could not think "of any exception where either hereditary constitution or environment has been the only factor responsible for physical differences".

The science of genetics suggests that the hereditary differences among populations of a single species are the results of the action of two sets of processes. On the one hand the genetic composition of isolated populations is constantly but gradually being altered by natural selection and by occasional changes (mutations) in the material particles (genes) which control heredity. Populations are also affected by fortuitous changes in gene frequency and by marriage customs. On the other hand crossing is constantly breaking down the differentiations so set up.

This sentence was made clearer by suggestions from Steinberg, who proposed inserting in the first part of it the words "among populations of one species" and in the second part "the genetic composition of".

On the one hand, the genetic composition of isolated populations is constantly but gradually being altered by natural selections and by occasional changes (mutations) in the material particles (genes) which control heredity.

According to Needham, the order should be reversed, "since natural selection works upon a body of genotypic and phenotypic characteristics which have been brought into being by mutations". He added: "Would it not be wise to include some forms of words here which would leave room for cytoplasmic inheritance of some kind; detected now by so many western workers as well as in the controversial work of Lysenko and his school?"

Trevor doubts whether (the adverb "constantly" in this sentence is enough. It might imply "rapid change" whereas "the opposite case might be argued with some force by certain anthropologists". He suggests that this adverb be replaced by "slowly" or "at a slow rate". Morant thinks the same. Similarly, Luria proposes that the last words of the same sentence run as follows: "changes (mutations) in the structure and organization of the genetic materials that control heredity", since, as he explains, "this formulation would be more explicitly inclusive of mutational changes in ploidy, chromosomal organization and cytoplasmic determinants of heredity".

Le Gros Clark sees no need to establish an antithesis between the sentence describing the causes of racial differentiation and the sentence recalling that constant crossbreedings continually modify the populations thus formed. For this reason he proposes that a mere "However" should replace "On the one hand . . . on the other hand."

The hereditary characters to be used in the classification of human groups, the limits of their variation within these groups, and thus the extent of the classificatory subdivisions adopted may legitimately differ according to the scientific purpose in view.

This sentence brings from Mather this brief comment: "Race surely is a genetical notion depending on genetic affinity. Any or all characters may be used in the endeavour to trace this affinity. This sentence virtually says that race has no one meaning or even set of closely approximating meanings. This would be expected at the phenotype level in man, even if there were some genetical justification for the notion."

SECTION 3

This section, as a whole, prompts Howells to the following reflection: "The polemic tone also seems to be the reason for the somewhat overdrawn (as it seems to me) statement of paragraph 3. One thing that I miss in the Statement as a whole is the notion of a *population* as the only thing which can become and constitute a race. This idea appears in paragraph 2, where it belongs, as the object of the influences there described. But then in paragraph 3 it seems to me to be completely flouted and negated by the zealous attempt of that paragraph to deal with the well-known error in the use of 'race'. E.g. 'Muslims and Jews are no more races than are Roman Catholics and Protestants; nor are people who live in Iceland or Britain . . .'. This seems to me to say that there is no 'racial' difference, let us say, between Jews and Protestants which is greater than that between Protestants and Roman Catholics, whereas there is evidence, historical (see Seltzer) and genetic (see Rife) that this is not so. Also, while it is quite correct to say that one would not speak of the Icelanders as a race, nevertheless Iceland would seem to be the ideal *population* which might eventually give rise to a distinct racial type, both via genetic isolation and selection in a special environment. I.e. in making one statement of broad correctness, paragraph 3 seems to me to destroy the germ of another idea of great importance for the *understanding* of race. If it were possible to have defined race a little more fully as a truly *biological* population rather than a social one, then it might be possible to deal with that great fallacy (of the 'French race', etc.) by showing how it does *not* coincide with the biological group which constitutes the prerequisite of a race, *without* making a statement which can leave doubts in the minds of a great many people."

National, religious, geographical, linguistic and cultural groups do not necessarily coincide with racial groups; and the cultural traits of such groups have no demonstrated connexion with racial traits.

Lipschutz would like the order changed and to put "cultural groups" first, because, as he explains, these different groups should be "subordinated to the idea of 'cultural', in order to be compared with 'racial' ".

Beaglehole wonders if this same sentence "is not likely to be a confusing way of stating a negative relationship. By saying that 'national, etc., groups' do not necessarily coincide with racial groups, the statement implies that national, etc., groups may and sometimes do, perhaps even often, coincide with racial groups. *But I should think that national, etc. groups very rarely* coincide with racial groups, as racial groups are defined elsewhere in the statement". Therefore, Beaglehole would like the sentence to read: "National, etc., groups *rarely* coincide with racial groups". He emphasizes that: "The key word here is obviously 'rarely', and if this word 'rarely' is used then the examples in paragraph 3 and the concluding sentence of paragraph 3 fall naturally into place in supporting the first sentence of this paragraph."

Concerning the same sentence, Darlington writes: "Of course not. But, as everybody knows, they create isolation of the kind which (as paragraph 2 points out) determines in due course the formation of races. To give the smaller part of the truth and conceal the larger is not very helpful to beginners. Still less helpful is it to conclude that Jews and Englishmen and Icelanders are not races. They are three good examples (again as described in paragraph 2) of the effects of inbreeding in groups of common origin in producing races in man. Indeed what are the 'two or more races within the same major groups' referred to in paragraph 4 if these are not such races? The Muslims, as the Committee must surely be aware, are not an example of an inbred community of common origin at all."

Americans are not a race, nor are Frenchmen, nor Germans; nor ipso facto is any other national group. Muslims and Jews are no more races than are Roman Catholics and Protestants....
In the first draft of the text, the English were cited among peoples who do not strictly constitue a race. Trevor criticizes this example: "I should not oppose the sentence if it ran thus: 'Americans are not a race, nor are Frenchmen or Germans', and stopped there. The American example is, surely, almost self-evident, even if one leaves Negroes and Indians out of the picture. Our Chairman in Paris, Professor Vallois, has indicated the racial heterogeneity of the French in his little book *Anthropologie de la population française* (Didier, Toulouse and Paris, 1943)—see especially page 119. Dr. Morant has likewise demonstrated that of the Germans in *The Races of Central Europe*, the preface of which was written by Professor Haldane (London, Allen and Unwin, 1939)—see especially pages 105-6, 112-13 and 136-40.

"In point of fact, the situation is rather different in this country. In comparison with the populations of most continental countries, the English—note that I do not say 'British'—are, and indeed have been since Tudor times, remarkably homogeneous. This opinion is based on a fairly large body of data recently studied by my wife and myself and still unpublished. I am sure that Dr. Morant, who knows more about living and dead Englishmen than anybody else, would agree with me here. In the Middle Ages our town communities were

44

as heterogeneous as one could imagine, but, for reasons too involved to go into here, I do not believe that the modern English (who resemble a pre-Saxon element in Britain) are descended from them.

"I should like to persuade my colleagues of the substance of these views, which I realize are not the popularly held ones but are true all the same. If they demur, I shall have to dissociate myself from the part of the sentence in question to which I object. If the example is intended only as an illustration, then I think there would be no harm in making the slight alteration I propose, since it can be supported by evidence, whereas the suggested racial heterogeneity of the English cannot."

Le Gros Clark would like the words "simply because of their religious views" to be added to the sentence, because "the ordinary man in the street does not necessarily think of a Jew as a man who practises a certain religion. Rightly or wrongly he assigns to the Jews (as a group) certain physical traits which he imagines distinguish them from other groups (even if they are not what are sometimes termed 'practising Jews')".

According to Frota-Pessoa, "it would be better to make clear that it is wrong to consider such groups as races if we settle our classification upon cultural characters, but that it is perfectly correct to talk about the American race (for instance, in opposition to the Mexican race), provided that we base our statement on the genetical differences existing between the respective populations."

. . . nor are people who live in Iceland or Britain or India, or who speak English or any other language, or who are culturally Turkish or Chinese and the like, thereby describable as races.

Le Gros Clark is not sure "what culturally Turkish means", and thinks that the allusion to those who are culturally Chinese "may confuse the casual reader, since it so happens that the people who are culturally Chinese do comprise a group whose physical characters appear (to the ordinary man in the street) to be rather distinctive".

Walter Landauer recommends adding to this section the following: "There is no proof that racial traits have had significant influence on cultural developments within the boundaries of any state or nation."

Concerning these words, Lenz observes: "The statement that national, religious, geographical, linguistic and cultural groups do not necessarily coincide with racial groups seems to me to be an understatement. Such differences do not generally coincide with racial differences, and certainly not as far as civilized European peoples are concerned. On the other hand, I do not consider it accurate to maintain that 'the cultural traits of such groups have no demonstrated connexion with racial traits'. If the word 'connexion' is used in the sense of 'correlation', the statement is definitely incorrect. From the purely empirical point of view, there are obvious correlations between the cultural and racial traits of human groups, and more particularly with regard to primitive cultural groups.

"I think I am right in assuming that Unesco is primarily concerned to show that Jews are not specifically different from the other members of the communities in which they life. In my opinion, too. there is no such specific difference between Jews and other persons. Nevertheless, Jews in general do differ from the other members of the communities in which they live, even racially, that is, by their inherited traits. I suggest that Jews should be considered as belonging to the European group. The term 'Asiatics', which Rathenau, among others, applied to the Jews, is misleading. The Jews, of course, have most of their genes in common with the other members of the communities in which they live. What is unevenly distributed among different civilized peoples and different social groups is not racial types as such but genes. I therefore suggest that, instead of applying the term 'race' to human groups, it would be better to interpret it as the sum total of the hereditary traits of man or group of men."

Lastly, Mather pointed out that "the people living in one country or speaking one language, etc., could be a race (e.g. Red Indians perhaps were); they need not be, however, and it so happens that in general they are not."

SECTION 4

On this section Coon made the following comments:
"Most physical anthropologists are no longer interested

46

in classifying races, and social anthropologists know no more about it than physicists or obstetricians. The physical anthropologists who work on this subject have all, to my knowledge, rejected the 150-year-old skin colour classification as inadequate. The Statement's paragraph 4 is therefore, in my opinion, incorrect. Physical anthropologists have not agreed on a basis of classification. My own system, on two functional axes, evolutionary status and specialization for thermal regulation, is relatively new and I do not know whether it will be eventually accepted or not."

Such a classification does not depend on any single physical character, nor does, for example, skin colour by itself necessarily distinguish one major group from another.

Darlington's comment is: "Agreed. But skin colour is, as we say in experimental breeding, a good *marker*. Pure black men are never found to be of exclusively European ancestry. Hence certain conclusions can be, and I think always will be, drawn from the colour of men by those who keep their eyes open. Whether the right conclusions are drawn will depend on our views in the next paragraph."

Furthermore, so far as it has been possible to analyse them, the differences in physical structure which distinguish one major group from another give no support to popular notions of any general "superiority" or "inferiority" which are sometimes implied in referring to these groups.

It was Le Gros Clark who proposed the present text of this sentence in place of the committee's: "From the morphological point of view, moreover, it is impossible to regard one particular race as 'superior' or 'inferior' to another," which was also criticized by many of our correspondents, especially the use of the word "morphological". "In so far as the physical traits characteristic of the different major groups are adaptive features," says Le Gros Clark, "then *in those particular respects* each group is presumably superior in its particular environment." The same idea is expressed by Coon: "Races are clearly superior and inferior to each other

47

under given circumstances. A jet black Sudanese is superior, in the Sudan, to a pink-skinned European. An Eskimo is superior in Greenland to nearly anyone. An Iraqi river dweller is superior to an American who would die in two weeks of infectious diseases if forced to drink raw Euphrates water."

Frota-Pessoa suggests that "this sentence should be substituted by an explanation more adequate to the subject, making clear the following points:

"1. To state that one race is superior to another is a judgment of value, which science can approve only when the criterion for such a judgment is objective. For this purpose it is essential that the attribute to be judged be well determined. There is no positive sense in stating simply that race A is superior to race B. It may be superior in relation to certain attributes, and inferior in relation to others. But if we say that race A is superior to race B, in the particular sense of being more resistant to tuberculosis, then it is within the field of science to decide whether the statement is true or not.

"2. As to the adaptive characters, the superiority of one race in relation to another ought to be reckoned after taking into account its environment. Supposing that there is more hereditary resistance to a certain tropical disease in the Negro race, this superiority is effective for inhabitants of Africa, but it has no practical value for the inhabitants of Europe, where the climate is not consistent with such a disease. The black colour of the skin probably is a point of superiority in the case of people living in tropical regions, who need a better protection against the sun. White colour, however, allows a better synthesis of vitamin D, and is probably superior for the inhabitants of regions with little sunshine.

"3. The presence in a certain race of some characters resembling those of anthropoids does not ensure that such a race is phylogenetically more primitive. The primitiveness of one character judged in accordance with comparative anatomy does not imply the primitiveness of other characters of the same individual, and still less any general phylogenetic primitiveness. It is, therefore, impossible, in the present state of science, to range different races according to their degrees of general primitiveness."

Broadly speaking, individuals belonging to different major groups of mankind are distinguishable by virtue of their physical characters, but individual members, or small groups, belonging to different races within the same major groups grade into each other, and the physical traits by which they and the races within them are characterized overlap considerably. With respect to most, if not all, measurable characters, the differences among individuals belonging to the same race are greater than the differences that occur between the observed averages for two or more races within the same major group.

Miss Tildesley objects to the wording of the last sentence of the paragraph and proposes the following version: "Greater differences occur between individuals belonging to the same race than between the observed averages for races within the same major group."

SECTION 5

Birdsell finds that the "statement under heading No. 5, concerning the mental characteristics of human races, is admittedly an up-to-date summary of the current position". However, he discerns in it certain weaknesses "from an educational point of view". He writes: "It seems to me that its very fullness of statement, together with the multiple qualifications, will leave non-professional readers with the idea that after all, time may reveal that important differences in innate intelligence probably will be demonstrated between racial populations. I wonder if a clearer position might not be established with three simple introductory ideas: (a) so-called intelligence tests are not a measure of differences of innate or biologically endowed intelligence between groups which differ culturally; (b) to date, no psychological tests have been devised which are culture-less in content on both an explicit and implicit level; and (c) no method has yet been divised to measure the innate intelligence of the individual."

To Mather, this section appears "to a great extent a statement of ignorance about genetical differences in

mental capacity". He adds: "I would agree that we
know little about it, but this ignorance must not be
used as a basis for saying that average differences do
not exist between populations in the mental capacity
of their constituent individuals."

Mayr finds this section "exceedingly weak" and is
afraid that it "may pull down the entire, otherwise so
admirable, Statement".

Most anthropologists do not include mental characteris-
tics in their classification of human races.

Lenz, on the other hand, thinks that "every attempt
to restrict racial differences to physical differences is
both arbitrary and scientifically unjustifiable. Linnaeus
expressly included psychical differences in his diagnoses.
Psychical hereditary differences are much more important than physical differences".

When intelligence tests, even non-verbal, are made on
a group of non-literate people, their scores are usually
lower than those of more civilized people. It has been
recorded that different groups of the same race occupy-
ing similarly high levels of civilization may yield consi-
derable differences in intelligence tests. When, however,
the two groups have been brought up from childhood in
similar environments, the differences are usually very
slight. Moreover, there is good evidence that, given
similar opportunities, the average performance (that is
to say, the performance of the individual who is repre-
sentative because he is surpassed by as many as he
surpasses), and the variation round it, do not differ
appreciably from one race to another.

Luria is not satisfied with this paragraph: "There
appears to be an inadequate realization of the present
limitations to any operational approach to comparative
intelligence testing in groups with different language and
different structure of civilization. Intercultural stan-
dardization of tests, particularly at the international
level, is at best unsatisfactory. This should be emphasized in qualifying the statement on the results of intelligence tests as related to level of civilization."

Mayr, who considers the second half of this section
the weakest passage in the whole Statement, asks for
something less positive: "I think I know the literature

quite well but I fail to have encountered any work that would permit the exceedingly positive opinions embodied in the two last sentences of the second section of paragraph 5. I do not know of a single experiment where two random groups, belonging to two different races, have been brought up from childhood in similar environments, and have been tested subsequently. All cases known to me were selected samples, not random samples. However, no proof has been submitted that there are any such differences between races and populations, and I would consider it infinitely more objective to state the two sentences negatively, that is, 'No evidence has been submitted that . . .'."

This is also the opinion of Stern, who suggests: "Would not the relatively few and limited studies relevant to this sentence, rather call for a wording somewhat like 'there is no good evidence that . . . the performance differs appreciably from one race to another'?"

Krogman thinks that this paragraph might be omitted, as also the last paragraph in the section "I have," he says, "a feeling of 'special pleading' in this entire section, once the basic point of paragraph 1 is established."

Herskovits misses here "the fine hand of a cultural anthropologist, not included in the group that drew up the Statement . . . for 'race occupying similarly high levels of civilization' it seems to me that it would be much better to substitute 'race having similar cultures'. This again would not lay the committee open to the assumption of judging differential values in cultures, something that was not intended."

Even those psychologists who claim to have found the greatest differences in intelligence between groups of different racial origin, and have contended that they are hereditary, always report that some members of the group of inferior performance surpass, not merely the lowest ranking member of the superior group, but also the average of its members. In any case, it has never been possible to separate members of two groups on the basis of mental capacity, as they can often be separated on a basis of religion, skin colour, hair form or language. It is possible, though not proved, that some types of innate capacity for intellectual and emotional responses are commoner in one human group than in another, but it is certain that, within a single group, innate capacities vary as much as, if not more than, they do between different groups.

This paragraph, as was to be expected, aroused the keenest discussion between the scientists consulted. Muller subjected it to detailed criticism and his remarks must be quoted in full, since they represent an important trend of ideas: "I quite agree with the chief intention of the article as a whole, which, I take it, is to bring out the relative unimportance of such genetic mental differences between races as may exist, in contrast to the importance of the mental differences (between individuals as well as between nations) caused by tradition, training and other aspects of environment. However, in view of the admitted existence of some physically expressed hereditary differences of a conspicuous nature, between the averages or the medians of the races, it would be strange if there were not also some hereditary differences affecting the mental characteristics which develop in a given environment, between these averages or medians. At the same time, these mental differences might usually be unimportant in comparison with those between individuals of the same race."

In a second letter Muller explains his dissent still more clearly: "Whatever may have been said on the matter in the correspondence which the committee has had with other geneticists I am convinced that if a questionnaire were sent to geneticists in general, or to a group of let us say 20 or 30 representative geneticists, the great majority would agree with my criticism, even though anthropologists might not do so. It would therefore be unfair for the committee to imply that the passage in question had the approval of geneticists. It happens that your committee has consulted a few geneticists who even though justly eminent, represent a much more extreme point of view on this matter than that prevalent among geneticists in general, or among geneticists who are regarded by their colleagues as having done outstanding work. Moreover, it is difficult for me to believe that most of even that group of geneticists which your committee has already consulted would concur in the particular passage under dispute if they were asked specifically about this point and had also read my protest concerning it.

"To the great majority of geneticists it seems absurd to suppose that psychological characteristics are subject to entirely different laws of heredity or development than other biological characteristics. Even though the former characteristics are far more influenced than the latter by environment, in the form of past experiences, they must have a highly complex genetic basis. It is well known that there are rare genetic differences which have a tremendous influence on mentality so as to cause, for example, idiocy, and by all previous genetic experience we must conclude that there are very many more genes causing slighter differences, which are recognized with greater difficulty or not at all because of the obscuring effect on them of the environmental differences which occur simultaneously. Psychological comparisons of fraternal and identical twins have provided one type of empirical evidence in support of this conclusion. Since now there are these very abundant *individual* differences affecting psychological traits it would be extremely strange if there were not also differences, in the frequencies of such genes, between one major race and another, in view of the fact that there are such pronounced differences in the frequencies of genes affecting physically and chemically expressed traits. That would surely be the attitude of the great majority of geneticists.

"The above by no means implies that these genetic differences in psychological traits cannot be largely overridden by environmental influences. Moreover, the affects of different traditions, training and environment in general are so great that we have at present no way of ascertaining just what these genetic differences are or what the magnitude of their affect on one or another psychological trait would be if all the peoples had the same cultural and material background. No doubt the differences in some psychological respects are much greater than in others, just as two peoples may differ very much in skin colour and very little in height. It is indeed quite likely that if tests could be made with the requisite exactitude, some peoples would be found to have the genetic basis for a greater development than others of certain psychological traits in regard to which they had been supposed to be particularly deficient. That is, the differences in their extra-genic background would in some cases be found to have worked in the opposite direction from those in their genetic composition, and so to have given an entirely false impression of the latter. At present, therefore, we have no scientific data for assessing the latter. It would be quite proper to state this. Yet, at the same time, we do have every reason to infer that genetic differences, and even important ones, probably do exist between one living racial group of men and another, and our statement should not imply the contrary.

"It would be a tragic mistake to suppose that the above realistic, scientific view leads to the conclusion that race prejudices are justified. It is highly important, especially at this crisis in the relations between peoples, for the committee to give the correct argument against these prejudices. The essential points are that the different racial groups (a) are enough alike genetically, (b) are capable of being so much influenced in mental development by cultural and other environmental factors, and (c) contain such important individual genetic differences for psychological traits within each one of them, that all of them are capable of participating and co-operating fruitfully in modern civilization (as has also been empirically demonstrated). It also follows from this that all men should be given equal opportunities, equal civil rights, and the privilege of being judged and treated entirely as individuals without reference to their racial origin. There is, further, the important point that the evidence to date indicates that genetic mixing between the different existing races of man involves no important biological incompatibility and does not lead to any kind of biological inferiority which would be expressed in a psychological or any other way. (Certain special adaptations to given climates and ways of life would, it is true, tend to be reduced, but under modern civilization most of these needs can readily be met by artificial means.)

"Undoubtedly the truth of the point of view above expressed will some time be generally recognized. It would be very unfortunate if in the meantime a statement had been drawn up by the committee which made the argument for the fair treatment of one race by another depend upon the spurious notion that they are identical in the genetic basis of psychological traits. It is to be hoped that the committee, then, will reconsider this matter so as not to have its pronouncement open to attack. It is important not to weaken the good influence which a statement by the committee could have, in helping to ease the very dangerous race tensions and race prejudices so threatening the security of the world of today and tomorrow."

Sturtevant quite agreed with Muller on that point as appears from a letter he wrote to him of which he sent us a copy: "I agree with your point of view on the matter of inherent differences between human individuals and races. I have felt for some time that some of the arguments for racial equality were so obviously contrary to genetical experience as to be positively harmful—even when I approved of the conclusions drawn as to desirable social aims.

"There is excellent evidence for the existence of individual differences in mental characteristics—all the way from purely sensory differences such as colour-blindness to severe mental derangements such as phenylketonuria. On general grounds there can be little question that less easily analysed genetic differences occur in all sorts of mental properties. There can also be little question that there are at least statistical differences between races in such genes.

"But the conclusion to be drawn is not that one race is better than another—the sensible conclusion is that the two are different and that the members of each one are different one from another. The reasonable course for society to pursue is to give these diverse individuals every opportunity to develop their individual potentialities. There are probably many individuals—in who knows which races—who have the genetic potentialities to accomplish cultural advances of kinds that are not likely to be achieved without making use of combinations of genes that happen not yet to have been given a social opportunity. This, I think, is the genetical argument for point 4.

"In short, a recognition of the existence of inherited individual differences is necessary for an enlightened approach to racial problems. It is incumbent on the geneticist, at this point, to insist on the importance of the environmental element in the determination of human behaviour; for clearly a given genetic composition may lead to very different kinds of individuals in different environments, but the argument that environment is the *sole* determinant is something that every competent geneticist must protest against."

Fisher's attitude towards the facts stated in this paragraph is the same as Muller's and Sturtevant's, but this is how he puts his objections: "As you ask for remarks and suggestions, there is one that occurs to me, unfortunately of a somewhat fundamental nature, namely that the Statement as it stands appears to draw a distinction between the body and mind of men, which must, I think, prove untenable. It appears to me unmistakable that gene differences which influence the growth or physiological development of an organism will ordinarily *pari passu* influence the congenital inclinations and capacities of the mind. In fact, I should say that, to vary conclusion (2) on page 5, 'Available scientific knowledge provides a firm basis for believing that the groups of mankind differ in their innate capacity for intellectual and emotional development,' seeing that such groups do differ undoubtedly in a very large number of their genes."

In Darlington's opinion, this paragraph is far from proving that populations do not differ in their innate capacities. "But what members of the committee doubt that peoples differ in this respect? Would it not therefore be more candid and more instructive to say: 'we believe that peoples differ in the kind of innate capacity they show'? If the committee are not satisfied that, for example, the people of Wales have greater innate capacities in some directions than the people of England and less in others, they should visit these islands and study the people themselves. They should consider music, poetry and religion in the two countries. They should examine the Welsh population in London and its professions."

Genna also contests this paragraph: "It is argued that contemporary scientific knowledge does not justify admission of the existence of psychological racial differences; but that does not surely mean that our knowledge confirms the *non*-existence of elementary psychological differences at least among the major groups."

Coon observes that "racial differences in intelligence may or may not occur". He believes that "the effort to belittle them on humanitarian grounds is a tactical mistake because, if someone should prove them, you are out on a limb. Human beings deserve treatment as equals because of their quality of being human, and not because no one has yet found a way to prove some less brilliant than others. In a democratic nation the right to vote is not based on an IQ test and the same should be true in a democratic world".

Landauer would like this paragraph deleted: "As I understand it, the tenor of the first three paragraphs is that, if differences in mental traits exist between races, our present techniques are inadequate to demonstrate them. With this I would 'entirely agree." But he finds the last part of this paragraph upsetting: "If it is *'not proved'* that some types, etc., are commoner in one people than in another, how can it be *'certain'*, etc.? It seems to me also somewhat objectionable to concede the first part as a possibility and then to overrule it by appeal to total variance. Theoretically at least a difference in *one* or *a very few* traits *might* be of the utmost importance in evolution, social affairs, etc."

"The statement as to 'innate capacities' is definitely non-operational," writes Luria, "since innate capacities are not amenable now to measurement at the level of national groups, particularly because of the preponderant role of 'cultural heredity' in any human community."

Mayr finds the last sentence in this paragraph "vague" and points out that "it is a statistically unsound proposition. It implies that the total variants of different groups are smaller than the variants of single groups, which is obvious nonsense. What is meant, and what should have been said, is that the differences among individuals of a single group may be greater than the differences between the means of different groups".

Muller contends that this is a scientifically unproven statement: "I would add that, although not *proved,* this possibility would seem a very likely one by analogy with the physical differences, since there is no scientific ground for distinguishing between the kind of biological basis possessed by morphologically visible characteristics and by mental ones. Now when we say that there is a given difference in any hereditary characteristics we of course mean a difference in the hereditary material which affects the *development* of that characteristic. It

57

is only the capacity for development of a characteristic that is ever inherited, never the characteristic as such. That is, for the proper definition of that capacity the environment in question must also be specified. In view of all this it seems to me that it is entirely incorrect to say, as in point 2 of the summary: 'Available scientific knowledge provides no basis for believing that the groups of mankind differ in their innate capacity for intellectual and emotional development.' For this passage would imply that, given the same environment, the same degree and type of development would be attained by the average (or median) of all races."

Snyder, in a letter to Muller (20 May 1952) replies to the latter's criticism of this part of the Statement. He says: "The statement you quote on page 1 of your letter appears quite sound; and it does not seem to me (nor to others to whom I have shown it) to say or to imply 'that there *are* scientific data for concluding that all races are alike in regard to the genes that lie at the basis of the development of psychological characteristics.' To say that 'There is no basis for believing that A and B are different' is not the same as to say 'there *is* basis for believing that A and B are identical.'"

The normal individual, irrespective of race, is essentially educable. It follows that his intellectual and moral life is largely conditioned by his training and by his physical and social environment.

Mayr considers it "an outright falsehood to say that 'his intellectual and moral life is largely conditioned by his training'. I grant this for the moral life, but what is meant by 'intellectual life'? All the available evidence indicates that a high component of intellectual capacity is genetically fixed. If something else than intellectual capacities is meant, it should be stated."

"It does not appear evident" writes Buzzati-Traverso, "that the conditioning of the intellectual and moral life of the individual is a necessary consequence of his educability." He therefore proposes to drop the words "it follows".

Concurring in this suggestion, Landauer adds: "What is meant, I suppose, is that the great majority of 'normal' people (i.e. people who are not Voltaires or Rousseaus) are forced into a pattern by education, training,

58

etc. I don't quite see why that is added to what goes before. If the point is that social and other *mores* are probably more important than genetic traits in creating differences of behaviour between races, it could perhaps be expressed in a better way than it is now."

The following is Darlington's comment on the subject: "This means that (in the opinion of the committee) the majority of individuals in all races are not imbeciles, or at least not essentially imbeciles. The word 'essentially' here presumably means 'genetically'. . . . Do the committee deny that intellectual and moral life are also 'largely conditioned' by heredity and subject to racial differences? Apparently they do."

It often happens that a national group may appear to be characterized by particular psychological attributes. The superficial view would be that this is due to race. Scientifically, however, we realize that any common psychological attribute is more likely to be due to a common historical and social background, and that such attributes may obscure the fact that, within different populations consisting of many human types, one will find approximately the same range of temperament and intelligence.

"Why superficial?", asks Darlington. "I believe the methods of genetic study, the analysis of twins, the considerations, mathematical, cytological and experimental, of the genetics of populations and the effects of inbreeding and outbreeding, are not superficial. Some people find them quite penetrating—and also quite difficult.

"Are we to suppose that the difference between 'the common historical and sociological background', for example of the Patahna and the Bengali, has no genetic component? Are we to suppose that the intellectual and temperamental differences between the Brahmin and the Untouchable, or between Muslim, Jewish and Christian inhabitants of Palestine, living together in the same country for centuries, have no genetic basis and nothing to do with race?

"When the Statement suggests that within different populations 'one will find the same range of temperament and intelligence', does it really mean that idiots and angels are found with equal frequency in Milan and Naples? Or does it mean that samples of the populations of the two cities would give equivalent or similar results if tested in their innate capacities for the varied occupations of civilized life? Here is an experiment that Unesco might undertake. Clearly no Italian Government would undertake it because it would know the result in advance."

To Mayr, "it appears as if 'psychological attributes' in the first sentence is considered as identical with 'temperament and intelligence' of the last sentence. Again, this indicates to me fuzzy thinking".

Quoting the two last paragraphs in Section 5, Snyder writes to Muller: "These paragraphs appear also to dispose of Saller's concern (quoted with approval by Nachtsheim in his letter of 14 March) that the possibility of the existence of genetically based 'psychic' differences among races must be left open, lest the authors of the Statement later be forced to retract their words...."

"Your argument (8 April, page 2) that 'the existence of data proving substantial differences (among races) in the case of physical traits of varied kinds makes the inference very probable that significant differences in regard to the genes for psychological traits exist also' is valid in one sense, but misleading in another. That is, it does seem highly probable that there may be racial differences in the frequencies of such rare major genes as those responsible for phenylketonuric amentia, amaurotic idiocy, etc. But it seems very improbable that the racial distribution of genes of this class are 'significant' in establishing racial group differences that have any meaning for the layman, however interesting and important they may be from a theoretical standpoint. In so far as this thesis of yours may be intended to apply to 'psychological traits' within the range of non-pathological variability, I think it is hardly tenable. Some of the reasons for this scepticism are outlined in the chapter by David and myself in *Social Psychology at the Crossroads*, and Dobzhansky argues along similar lines in his contribution to *Evolutionary Thought in America*."

The scientific material available to us at present does not justify the conclusion that inherited genetic differences are a major factor in producing the differences between the cultures and cultural achievements of different peoples or groups. It does indicate, on the contrary, that a major factor in explaining such differences is the cultural experience which each group has undergone.

Lenz entirely disagrees with this assertion:

"Contrary to what is stated in this paragraph, it seems to me that there is very strong evidence to show that genetic differences are a 'major factor' in producing differences between cultural groups. It is true that the 'history of cultural experience', that is to say the acquisition and transmission of cultural values, is of great importance from the point of view of tradition; but does it explain the decline and fall of civilizations such as the Greek civilization? The most obvious explanation of such a decline is the lack of selection, that is to say the inadequate propagation of hereditary traits which make possible the creation and preservation of cultural values. As a result of lack of selection, a people can, within a relatively small number of generations, degenerate so far that it is culturally much inferior to another people which it formerly excelled in that respect. In my opinion, the West is now moving in that direction. It is therefore both unjustifiable and courting disaster to invoke the cultural achievements of real or imaginary ancestors (such as the 'Aryans')."

Coon points out in this connexion that, "while races may not have affected culture, as far as we know, culture *has* affected race. Our reduction in teeth and jaw size is culturally induced, through cooking and other food-softening processes. Some have softened their food more than others, with correspondingly differential results.

"Furthermore there has undoubtedly been strong selection at play in certain countries to eliminate unsuitable skin types, while equally strong selection in the cold places has favoured the fat face and the small extremity. Culture, by making it possible for people to live in given environments and to attain certain numbers in these places, has subjected man to the force of such natural laws as those of Bergman, Allen and Gloger, along with the rest of the fauna".

SECTION 7

There is no evidence for the existence of so-called "pure" races.

On this point, Darlington writes: "Here we are back at the beginning again. In an outbreeding organism like man there are not pure races of the same character as in self-fertilized or parthenogenetic organisms. Nevertheless in certain racial situations, as in Hawaii, it would be foolish to overlook the fact that the Japanese, the Hawaians, and even the whites, are so-called pure races as compared with the offspring from crossing these races. It would be foolish to disregard the analogy with the Mendelian experiment in which one distinguishes between so-called F1, F2, backcross, and derivative, progeny."

Coon merely says: "The concept of the 'pure' race in a non-laboratory population is academic and pre-genetic."

In regard to race mixture, the evidence points to the fact that human hybridization has been going on for an indefinite but considerable time.

"The evidence," writes Darlington, "points to the fact that wide crossing has never before taken place on such a scale as during the last 400 years. Sea transport has brought the most extreme human types together for the first time. The hybridization that took place before the invention of navigation was obviously of a very different order from what happens now and anyone who attempted to write human history and neglect this fact might just as well repudiate all biology."

As there is no reliable evidence that disadvantageous affects are produced thereby, no biological justification exists for prohibiting intermarriage between persons of different races.

Darlington, remarking that this is an example "of the worst effects of reiterating the negative (presumably in

62

answer to an invisible antagonist", asks: "What is the alternative? Disadvantageous with respect to what? To non-breeding? To incest? Or to crossing with an absent number of the same race? And in what circumstances? In the home country of one race? Or of the other? Or of both? When the Fuegians crossed with Europeans there cannot be any doubt that the progeny were superior to both parent races for living in Tierra del Fuego. But we may doubt very much whether the progeny were superior to both for living in Europe. Different kinds of results have arisen from race crossing in all parts of the world. They show reliably and conclusively that the progeny are different in innate capacity from either parent of the so-called pure race and that these differences are sometimes advantageous and sometimes disadvantageous, to one or both in the circumstances obtaining. Simply because the innate capacities of all races of men, as of animals, are different, and are suited to different circumstances and habitats.

"There might therefore be a 'biological justification for prohibiting intermarriage' between races if intermarriage were not contrary to the habits of all stable communities and therefore in no need of discouragement."

Weinert writes about this section: "Whether there is any 'biological' justification for considering races to differ in value does not alter the fact that human beings themselves attach different values to their races. Consequently, half-castes always try to win recognition as members of a 'higher' race, but this the latter race generally denies them. In defence of prohibiting marriage between persons of different races, I should like to ask which of the gentlemen who signed the Statement would be prepared to marry his daughter to an Australian aboriginal, for example."

Howells suggests that at the end of the section a sentence be added "corresponding to the very last sentence of the conclusion, i.e., 'This is a purely social problem.' It is too easy for ordinary readers and non-legalistically-minded reporters of the 'Would-you-like-your-daughter-to-marry-a-Negro' kind, to miss the word 'biological' in front of 'justification'."

"By 'biological', I assume that 'morphological' is meant," writes Krogman. "I think that it should be recognized that there are possible physiological differences which, though not prohibiting intermarriage, may be deleterious. I refer to sickle cell anaemia, Cooley's anaemia, as examples."

Luria regrets the choice of words in this sentence. To avoid misconstruction, he proposes the following: "No biological knowledge exists that counterindicates inter-marriage...."

Le Gros Clark would like "other than social" to be inserted after "disadvantageous affects".

SECTION 8

We now have to consider the bearing of these statements on the problem of human equality. We wish to emphasize that equality of opportunity and equality in law in no way depend, as ethical principles, upon the assertion that human beings are in fact equal in endowment.

Beaglehole makes several reservations about this section:

"The sentence about the ethical principles of equality seems to me to be inadequate as it stands, particularly as this single sentence follows the rather pretentious first sentence, which reads: 'We now have to consider the bearing of these statements on the problem of human equality.' It is rather a negative remark that two ethical principles are not related to an assertion about the equal endowments of human beings. I feel that this summary sentence may create more doubts than it allays and, therefore, I would wish to see this sentence enlarged (though necessarily briefly) by some positive statement which would help the ordinary reader grasp the relationship that is sometimes asserted to exist between equal endowment and equality of opportunity, or, to help the ordinary reader grasp the fallacious reasoning which is believed by the drafters of the Statement to be the basis for the confusion between an ethical principle and a factual statement about biological equality of endowment."

Mayr thinks "the last sentence of paragraph 8 is bad. 'Equal in endowment' is a meaningless statement, nor is the term 'assertion' fortunate. What is presumably meant is 'upon the proof that human beings are in fact identical in endowment'."

Concerning this section, Sturtevant writes: "I think that Section 8 is an excellent formulation of the basic liberal attitude on the questions discussed in the Statement, and should like to see it more prominently placed. Were it not for the inclusion of this statement, the reader might infer that the essential argument for racial tolerance lies in the supposed absence of inherent genetic differences in mental properties. If it should be definitely established that such differences exist, much of the argument in the Statement would be invalidated; but Section 8 would still stand."

SECTION 9

According to Penrose "the conclusions presented in Section 9 simply tend to perpetuate misleading modes of thought. Unless continued belief in racial divisions of mankind is desired, Section 9 (a) is an unnecessary caution. In Section 9 (b) and Section 9 (c), 'groups' and 'single races' respectively are so vague that they render these statements of little value, and in Section 9 (e) such a phrase as 'crosses (mating or marriages) between members of relatively isolated populations' is surely better than 'race mixture'."

(a) *In matters of race, the only characteristics which anthropologists have so far been able to use effectively as a basis for classification are physical (anatomical and physiological).*

According to Genna, "if anthropologists do not use psychological differences in their classification of races, that is due not so much to the fact that those differences are lacking as to the difficulty of determining them and to the element of subjectivity inevitable in their evaluation".

Krogman writes: "Anatomical—yes. Physiological —limited. Do you include immunochemistry here? (serology)."

(b) *Available scientific knowledge provides no basis for believing that the groups of mankind differ in their innate capacity for intellectual and emotional development.*

65

As for Section 5, this corollary is the subject of many reservations.

Muller fears that the force of the whole Statement will be reduced if the point is maintained, and adds: "It is self-defeating to overshoot the mark or engage in inconsistencies in this manner. And it is highly important to get the main point across as unassailably as possible: the point that each individual should be judged for himself, that race prejudices are pernicious, and that equality of opportunity is a crying social need. In view of this, I sincerely hope that the above will be corrected."

.Here is how Fischer would word this point: "Available scientific knowledge provides a firm basis for believing that the groups of mankind differ in their innate capacity for intellectual and emotional development, seeing that such groups do differ undoubtedly in a very large number of their genes."

Mather agrees that "there is no final proof that groups of mankind differ in their average capacities (though obviously their constituent individuals so differ)", but he points out that "equally there is no proof that they do not differ". He concludes: "As stated, this paragraph is tendentious."

As for Landauer: "The Statement is unquestionably true as of now, but," he adds, "I would be most surprised if it were to remain true in the future. What makes it unreasonable to expect that genes for mental and emotional traits have distribution patterns similar to those of physical traits, e.g., blood groups?"

Stern proposes the following text for this corollary: "Scientific knowledge has not yet reached the state where it can state whether or not the (mental) differences are based, in addition to the established influences on man's physical and social environments, on differences in innate capacities."

Neel regrets that the committee did not word this paragraph more cautiously: "I feel," he writes, "that just as there are *relatively minor* physical differences between races, so there may well be *relatively minor* mental differences. The available psychological techniques are simply inadequate for evaluating the existence of such possible innate differences. I agree with the committee in minimizing the magnitude of these differences, and feel it is a laudable attempt to offset some

66

of the 'racisms' of the past. But as scientists do we really believe that the available data permit minimizing the differences clear out of existence? Why not alter (the paragraph) along these lines: 'It is possible that just as there are *relatively minor* physical differences between certain groups of mankind, so there are *relatively minor* mental differences, but available scientific knowledge provides no basis for believing that the groups of mankind differ significantly in their innate capacity for intellectual and emotional development.'"

Morant would more readily accept the proposition contained in this corollary with the following qualification: "It is possible, however, that all the groups are not exactly alike in such ways."

Mayr points out that in this corollary as in the one that follows, "differences in variance and differences between means are again confused".

(c) *Some biological differences between human beings within a single race may be as great as or greater than the same biological differences between races.* (Original text: *The biological differences between human beings within single races may be as great as the biological differences between races.*)

Genna denies the validity of this corollary: "Although it is true that biological differences between human beings within a single race may be of the same nature as differences between our race and another, it is also true that differences between races are usually greater than those which may exist between individuals of the same race."

Lenz' comment is: "The statement made in sub-paragraph (c) seems to be to overestimate the differences between races. In my opinion, the differences between human beings within single communities are substantially greater than the average differences between communities or 'races'. In civilized countries with millions of inhabitants there are hereditary differences of endowment, ranging from complete imbecility to the highest talent, and the hereditary differences of temperament and character are just as important. In this respect, I refer to the results of the investigations carried out by the psychologist, Gottschaldt, with regard to twins. The tremendous importance of hereditary differences of cha-

racter is strikingly shown by the research carried out by
the psychiatrist, Johannes Lange, who has given an
account of it in his famous book, *Verbrechen als Schick-
sal.*"

Buzzati-Traverso finds a "contradiction between what
is said here and what was said in the last words of
Point 4". He proposes adding at the end of the corollary
"within the major groups".

Landauer feels that this paragraph "implies *quanti-
tative* knowledge which in reality does not exist". "Is
it really certain," he asks, "that intra-population variability of mental traits is as great as or greater than that
between populations?"

Morant recommends caution in this corollary and suggests adding: "It is probable that this is the situation
in the case of all innate mental characters."

(d) *Vast social changes have occured that have not been
connected in any way with changes in racial type.
Historical and sociological studies thus support the
view that genetic differences are of little significance
in determining the social and cultural differences
between different groups of men.*

Darlington's comment is: "By this it is meant presumably that a governing class may be displaced by another class of the same race with vast effects. But are
we certain that this does not involve great genetic
changes, even physical changes readily visible—changes
of course in a very small section of society? In all the
first seven points the Statement has made use of the
existence of class (within-race) differences as a means
of casting doubt on between-race differences. Now it
implies that class differences are not important. Possibly, of course, the committee imagines that class and
caste differences, like race differences, have no serious
genetic basis, that we are all in the melting-pot together?
Yet if we turn back to the second paragraph, the only
one that is based on serious thought, we find that mating
barriers (such as occur between social classes) are
supposed to be the origin of genetic differentiation."

Mather urges circumspection: "There is at present
little evidence of direct effect of genetic differences on
social and cultural differences between groups (although
see Darlington on the subject of speech preferences).

But does this justify the statement that they are insignifiant?"

Stern proposes the following text: "Historical studies show that social and cultural differences can originate without underlying genetic differences of the populations concerned."

(e) *There is no evidence that race mixture produces disadvantageous results from a biological point of view. The social results of race mixture, whether for good or ill, can generally be traced to social factors.*

Sturtevant's opinion of this corollary is as follows: "The consequences of race mixture seem to me to be stated badly. There is a possible confusion between 'biological' and mental properties here. It is the general experience of those who have studied the results (at least beyond the first generation) of crosses between distinctly different strains of many kinds of organisms (including at least one mammal, the dog) that there is a strong tendency towards the production of physiologically inefficient individuals. The geneticist understands why this is so—and that understanding gives no grounds for expecting man to be an exception to the general rule. It is true that such crosses give the possibility of producing some individuals that are 'better' (in any specified respect) than any to be found in either parental race—but experience and theory are agreed that, after the first generation, these are much less likely to be found than are 'inferior' individuals. The result of these considerations is that, even on a purely physiological level, crosses between quite different races are not free of danger."

Kemp makes this comment: "No reports are available proving that crossing of human races should give biologically inferior offspring.... Race mixture may give rise to unfortunate selection, because it is often social and criminal persons from the higher race who mate with persons from a less civilized race. This has led to the mistaken conclusion, based on experience with such hybrids, that race mixture in itself is unfortunate.

"There is no reason to regard the pure human race as archetypical or particularly valuable.... It is therefore hardly possible to lay down general rules as to whether

69

crossing of races is advantageous or the reverse. If the races that have existed through several centuries can be supposed to have improved by selection, and therefore have a particularly harmonious and well-balanced constitution, race mixture can in certain cases be expected to lead to production of less harmonious and well-balanced types. On the other hand, race mixture may probably also cause production of successful combinations, which may give rise to quite new race types."

Needham asks for something more positive: "Couldn't one say that race mixture is positively advantageous, rather than not disadvantageous, as tending to unify humanity?"

OTHER SUGGESTED STATEMENTS

A few scientists, though convinced of the importance of giving the public a statement presenting, simply and succinctly, the main conclusions reached by the anthropologists and geneticists, were not entirely satisfied with the document submitted to them or which they had helped to draft. They therefore set to work to prepare statements free from the faults for which they criticized the Unesco Statement, and in line with their views of what a popular scientific document should be.

The versions that they have forwarded to us are extremely interesting. First and foremost, they reflect their authors' ideas on a number of important matters and often express most happily propositions which are difficult to formulate. We have therefore thought it well to reproduce these statements in this publication.

The document submitted by Lipschutz keeps very close to the committee's Statement. Those of Stewart and Dobzhansky present the question in a different form.

We conclude with two versions of the Statement proposed by L. C. Dunn, the committee's rapporteur, after considering our correspondents' observations. One of these versions seeks to take account of the most important comments and criticisms; the other recasts the various sections of the Statement in the form of a report, which, in Dunn's view, would be more suitable for the general public.

TWENTY-FOUR STATEMENTS ON RACE: A. LIPSCHUTZ

1. Scientists are generally agreed that all men belong to a *single species, Homo sapiens,* and are derived from a common stock, even though there is some dispute as to when and how different human groups diverged from this common stock.

71

2. The *concept of race* is unanimously regarded by anthropologists as a classificatory device providing a zoological, or biological, framework within which the various groups of mankind may be arranged. This classificatory device as shall be explained below, cannot be but arbitrary as all similar devices in science legitimately are.

3. From the point of view of anthropological science, "race" is reserved only for groups of mankind possessing *heritable physical characters different from those of other groups*. While such groups exist, it is also clear that, because of the complexity of human history during which miscegenation between groups with different heritable physical characters took place on a very ample scale, the overwhelming majority of human groups, or populations, cannot easily be fitted into a racial classification.

4. The *science of genetics* suggests that the hereditary differences are the result of the action of two sets of processes. On the one hand, isolated populations are constantly being altered by natural selection and by occasional changes (mutations) in the material particles (genes) which control heredity. Populations are also affected by fortuitous changes in gene frequency and by marriage customs and breeding structure. On the other hand, crossing is constantly breaking down the differentiations so set up. The new mixed populations in so far as they, in turn, become isolated, are subject to the same processes, and these may lead to further changes. The existence of different races is merely the result, considered at a particular moment in time, of the total effect of all these processes on the human species.

5. While physical differences between human groups are undoubtedly due to differences in the hereditary constitution, *differences of environment* in which the groups have been brought up, also cause considerable physical differences without altering necessarily the hereditary constitution. The differences of environment by which physical differences are caused, are both "natural" and "social".

72

6. The hereditary characters to be used in classification, the limits of variations permissible within the groups, and hence the size of the subdivisions to be adopted, may legitimately differ *according to the scientific purpose in view.*

7. Consequently, human races can be, and have been, *classified* by different anthropologists *in different ways.* But most agree in classifying the greater part of existing mankind in at least three large units, which may be called major groups (in French, *grand-races*): Asiatic or Yellow, European or White, African or Negro. Though admitting the convenience of this classification based on a single physical character as skin colour on account of its being evident for the man of the street and sanctified by tradition, it is from a scientific genetical point of view no more justified, or even less justified, than classifying mankind in four major groups in accordance with the four major blood groups.

8. Broadly speaking, individuals belonging to one of the three major groups of mankind—Yellow, White or Negro —are distinguishable from those of the other two major groups, by virtue of a whole *set of hereditary physical characters.* Individuals belonging to different racial subdivisions of the same major group are usually not so easily distinguishable as those belonging to different major groups, because the racial subdivisions grade into each other, and the physical traits by which they are characterized overlap considerably. But this applies even to the three major groups.

9. With respect to most, if not all, measurable physical characters, the differences among *individuals* belonging to the same racial subdivision are greater than the differences that occur between the observed averages for two or more racial subdivisions within the same major group.

10. From the point of view of physical anthropology, it is impossible to regard one particular race as *"superior"* or *"inferior"* to another.

11. There is no evidence for the existence of so-called *"pure" races.* Though we know the earlier human races

chiefly from skeletal remains and our knowledge is therefore limited, the evidence in regard to race mixture points to the fact that human hybridization has been going on for an indefinite but considerable time. Indeed, one of the processes of race formation and race extinction or absorption is by means of hybridization between human races. And there is no reliable evidence that disadvantages have been, or are, produced thereby, and no biological justification exists for prohibiting intermarriage between persons of different races.

12. *Cultural* groups, or national, linguistic, religious and geographical groups, do not necessarily coincide with *racial* groups. The cultural traits of such groups have no demonstrated causal connexion with hereditary racial traits. Americans are not a race, nor are Englishmen, Frenchmen, Spaniards, Turks or Chinese, nor any other national group. Muslims and Jews are no more races than are Catholics and Protestants. These cultural groups are not describable as races because each cultural group is composed of many different races. Serious errors are habitually committed when the term race is used in popular parlance; the term should never be used when speaking of such human cultural groups.

13. The scientific material available to us at present does not justify the conclusion that inherited racial differences are a factor in producing the differences between the cultures and cultural achievements of the different national, geographical or other human groups. It does indicate, on the contrary, that such differences are to be explained by many factors which interfere in the course of the history of the cultural experience of each group, factors which belong to *the realm of the sociologist, not of the biologist.*

14. Most anthropologists no longer try to include *mental characteristics* in their classification of human races. Studies within a single race have shown that both innate individual capacity, variable within the same social group, and variable environmental opportunity, mostly of a social order, determine the results of tests of intelligence and temperament, though their relative importance in each case also is variable.

15. When *intelligence tests*, even non-verbal, are made on a group of non-literate people, their scores are usually lower than those of more civilized people. On the other hand, different social groups of the same race occupying as a whole a high level of civilization may yield considerable differences in intelligence tests. When, however, these social groups have been brought up from childhood in similar environments, the differences are normally very slight. Moreover, there is good evidence that, given similar opportunities, the median performance—that is to say, the performance of the individual who is representative because he is surpassed by as many as he surpasses—and the variation around it, do not differ appreciably from one race to another.

16. The *standard of intellectual, emotional and moral values* is variable according to the variable exigencies of adaptation to environmental and social conditions of different groups within the same race, or of different races. Any mental test is consequently but a very elementary approach to the problem of the psychological attributes of different races. We consider this statement as fundamental for the just appreciation of the results of mental tests though it is not intended to underestimate their scientific importance.

17. The study of the *heredity of psychological characteristics* also is beset with difficulties. Even those psychologists who claim to have sometimes found the greatest differences in the *average* intelligence between groups of different racial origin, and have contended that these average differences are hereditary, always report that many members of the racial group of inferior performance not merely surpass the lowest ranking member of the racial group of superior performance, but *most of its members*. It has never been possible to separate, or characterize, members of two different racial groups on the basis of mental capacity, as they can be separated, or characterized, on a basis of skin colour or hair form, or on a basis of language or religion.

18. It is possible, though not proved, that some types of *innate capacity* for intellectual and emotional responses are commoner in one racial group than in another; but

it is certain that, within a racial group, innate capacities vary as much as, if not more than, they do between different racial groups.

19. We know that certain *mental diseases and defects* are hereditarily transmitted from one generation to the next. But we are less familiar with the part played by heredity in the mental life of normal individuals. The normal individual, *irrespective of race*, is essentially educable, and his intellectual and moral standards and life are largely conditioned by his natural and social environment and the corresponding training.

20. *National and social groups* may appear to be characterized by *particular psychological attributes* which in some cases may be even very striking. Since both national and social groups can be distinguished in some cases, and in some measure, also by hereditary physical characters as skin colour or blood groups, the superficial view would be that the particular psychological attributes of a national or social group are hereditary characters of the racial groups which compose the respective national or social groups, and that these supposedly hereditary psychological particularities are linked with hereditary physical characters as skin colour or blood groups. Scientifically, however, we realize that any particular psychological attribute of a national or social group is due to a particular historical and social background.

21. The latter is best shown by the fact that the psychological particularities both of national and social groups are subject to *rapid changes* in accordance with changes of the historical and social environment, a warlike tribe, for instance, being transformed into a sedentary peaceful group without any changes in the hereditary physical characters having taken place.

22. The existence of *hereditary physical differences between a privileged and a dependent social group* within the same national group does not denote racial "superiority" or "inferiority", or linkage of superior psychological characters with hereditary physical characters. It denotes interference or conquest by a foreign

76

racial group often culturally even inferior to the conquered racial group whose superior intellectual and emotional values become rapidly incorporated by the conquering racial groups, whereas these values become by and by corrupted in the conquered racial group. The conquering racial group may, for the purpose of defence of social privileges, also prohibit miscegenation with the conquered racial group, especially if the difference between the two competing racial groups as to visible hereditary physical characters is so pronounced, as for instance between Negro and white, that miscegenation represents an immediate danger for the upkeep of privileges.

23. The dogma of hereditary superior mental characteristics linked with hereditary physical characters is the very foundation of *"racial discrimination"*. The latter is an instrument for the defence of social privileges acquired by conquest of one racial group by another. Racial discrimination in modern society is made use of as a powerful means of *social discrimination* within the same national group or in a conquered foreign nation.

24. Equality of opportunity and equality in law, as *ethical principles* which are fundamental for the cultural development of mankind as a whole, in no way can be made dependant upon the assertion that human races or individual human beings are equal or non-equal in endowment.

We have thought it worth while to set out in a formal manner what is at present scientifically established concerning individual and group differences:
1. In matters of race, the only characteristics which anthropologists can effectively use as a basis for classification are physical (anatomical and physiological).
2. Available scientific knowledge provides no basis for believing that the different racial groups of mankind differ in their innate capacity for intellectual and emotional development.
3. The biological differences between human beings within single races may be as great as the biological differences between races.

4. Vast social changes have occurred which were not in any way connected with changes in racial type. Historical and sociological studies thus support the view that racial or genetic differences are of no significance in determining the social and cultural differences between different groups of men.
5. There is no evidence that race mixture as such produces disadvantageous results from a biological point of view. The social results of race mixture, whether for good or ill, can generally be traced to social factors.
6. There are no "superior" or "inferior" races neither physically nor mentally, and racial discrimination is but a means by which social discrimination and abuse of human groups of a different racial composure is made easier.

RACE: T. DALE STEWART

Historical records indicate that for a long time man has had a natural interest in the physical differences exhibited by the strange peoples whom he met. Thus, the early Egyptians in their wall paintings clearly differentiated their neighbours by both colour and form. As knowledge of the world increased and when science reached the stage of classifying living forms, it was a natural step for biologists to adopt some of the previously recognized subdivisions of mankind and to designate them as races. The scientists needed this device, however imperfect, in order to simplify their discussions of the subject. Naturally, these discussions included the meaning of the observable race differences, and specifically whether or not the races represented different levels of development in the evolutionary sense. Here the interpretations, like the men themselves, have varied. Scientists still carry on the discussion and they have not even decided the number of races. Such is the history of the original and true meaning of race. In this sense race has and is serving a practical purpose in science.

There is, however, a newer perverted meaning of race which falsely claims a scientific basis and which should be understood and combatted by everyone. Unscrupulous men from time to time have taken over the findings and speculations of scientists and have used them in altered form to better their own financial and political ends. Their misstatements, for example, aided Negro slavery in the United States and made it possible for the Nazi tyranny to expand rapidly. In this way exaggerated claims of racial superiority and inferiority came to be spread around and group hatreds were created. Race in this false sense can or does endanger the happiness of every individual.

Ignorance has also confused the true meaning of race. Cultural groups—political, religious, linguistic—are often spoken of erroneously as races. Obviously national groups such as the Americans and English are not biological races; they are not sufficiently different in appearance for the most part to constitute races. The same is true of religious groups like Catholics and Protestants, or of linguistic groups like the speakers of French and German. However, members of different races may be of the same nationality, the same religious denomination and speak the same language. A little thought will reveal the truth of this situation.

Since cultural and racial groups overlap, it is wrong and unjust to attribute group cultural status to race alone. Other factors, such as individual leadership, climate, geographical location and natural wealth, help forge the destinies of peoples. History shows that the cultural barbarians of one period can become the cultural leaders of a later period. This process has taken place in different races.

Cultures have mixed whenever and wherever they have come in contact; and likewise—regardless of race— the bearers of these cultures have mixed their bloods (the geneticists prefer to say "genes"). There is no biological evidence that this race mixture has been bad for mankind. Any social stigma attached to the mixed-breeds on account of their appearance is due to ignorance about the true meaning of race.

COMMENTS ON THE STATEMENT ON RACE CONCEPT: TH. DOBZHANSKY

The misuse of the word "race" by propagandists and

bigots has led the general public to distrust the idea of race altogether. It is often asked whether human races are ascertainable biological realities, or merely artificial groupings set by anthropologists for their own convenience. It is also asked to what extent the races of man are comparable to races which exist in other species, wild or domesticated, of animals and plants.

To answer the above questions, it is necessary to understand clearly the uses to which the concept of race is put in biology and in anthropology. Men are not all alike. As a matter of fact, everyday experience shows that every human individual differs from all others. Now, human diversity is studied scientifically in two different ways, which should complement each other. First, human diversity is observed, described, classified and catalogued. Secondly, the causes which bring about the diversity are analysed. The concept of race has originally been introduced as a category of classification, and it is still used for this purpose. On the other hand, races are biological populations, the nature of which must be examined.

For the classification purposes, it has often been found useful to regard individuals as variants of racial "types", to which they supposedly belong. Thus, individuals are sometimes spoken of as conforming to, or deviating from, the "types" of the Nordic, Mongolian, Melanesian, or other "races". The "type", however, is an abstraction. It is arrived at as a statistical average of traits in the sample of individuals actually studied. Such abstractions may be convenient for making a catalogue of human diversity. They are, however, misleading when confused with the living populations themselves.

The discovery of Mendel, that heredity is transmitted from parents to offspring not through "blood" but through genes, has shown that not the "types" but populations, i.e., the communities of individuals among whom marriages are concluded, are biological realities. Every human individual is a member of a population, but he has his own genetic constitution, not present in any other individual now living or having lived in the past (identical twins excepted). Human races are populations which differ from other populations in the incidence of certain genes. "Pure races", i.e., groups of individuals that are genetically uniform, can exist only in asexual species. "Pure races" in man are a myth, and attempts to describe the existing human populations as mixtures in different proportions of ancient "pure races" or "primary types" are fallacious.

Genetic differences between human populations are not absolute but relative. Race differences are compounded of the same elements, genes, in which individuals within a race often differ also. Furthermore, race differences may be of different orders. Populations which are geographically remote show greater genetic differences, on the average, than do populations which reside close together. It is, then, an arbitrary matter whether we divide mankind, for purposes of classification, into few or into many races. The number of races recognized by giving them names is a matter of convenience. Some anthropologists find it useful to distinguish only few major races, while others prefer finer subdivisions.

But while the number of races which we recognize is, thus, arbitrary, the existence of racial differences is an objectively ascertainable fact. Mankind is not a single breeding population, but a very complex system of breeding communities. These communities are maintained by geographic, cultural and economic barriers. And these communities are racially distinct when they differ in the frequencies of various hereditary traits. We set up races and give them names for the purpose of describing human diversity; racial differences between human populations are a biological reality.

Human races, just as races of other sexually reproducing organisms, are populations which differ in the frequencies of certain genes. To be sure, the genetic differences between human races are certainly less profound than between races in many other biological species. Races of man, as well as races of domesticated and wild animals and plants, are products of the evolutionary development. But the evolution of the human species has been influenced so profoundly by social and cultural history that the human biological nature cannot be understood except in connexion with his status, to use Aristotle's words, of "political animal".

REFORMULATION OF THE STATEMENT ON THE CONCEPT OF RACE: L. C. DUNN

Preamble

Race, in common usage, has had so many meanings and the resulting confusion has given so much opportunity for the operation of prejudice and persecution that it has become necessary to clarify and define the concept.

The Biological Concept of Race. Race as a biological term expresses the fact that there are populations of mankind like those of Africa and of Europe, for example, which differ in some of their hereditary characters. Anthropologists reserve the term "race" for those groups of mankind which regularly show extensive physical differences. Race, based on hereditary group differences has thus become a device for classifying and thereby describing in simpler terms the great variety existing in mankind.

Biologists also recognize racial differentiation as a part of the process by which local populations become fitted or adapted to their environment. Race as a biological category is thus based on the most universal of biological processes, that of evolution.

The Biological Position of Mankind. Anthropologists and zoologists are generally agreed that all living races of man belong to the single species, *Homo sapiens,* and have been derived by slow evolutionary change from a common stock. There is still some dispute as to the date and manner in which different human populations diverged from this common stock.

Race Classification. The racial classification of mankind can be and has been carried out in different ways by different anthropologists. Most agree in classifying the greater part of existing mankind on the basis of physical characters in at least three larger units, which have been referred to as white, black and yellow, although neither skin colour nor any other single physical character is a sufficient basis for the classification. It is impossible to regard any race as superior or inferior to another in the physical characters by which they differ.

Although members of different large groups are distinguishable by virtue of their physical characters, there is much overlapping even between the larger groups and particularly between races belonging to the same large group, so that it is usually not possible to distinguish a single individual as a member of a particular smaller group or race. With respect to most if not all measurable characters, the differences among individuals belonging to the same race are greater than the differences that occur between the observed averages for two or more races within the same major group. The hereditary characters to be used in classification, the limits of variation permissible within the groups and hence the size of the subdivisions to be adopted may legitimately differ according to the scientific purpose in view.

Race Formation. Physical differences between human groups arise in two ways. Some are due to the direct effects of the environment (such as degree of tanning of the skin, deliberate alterations of hair form, head shape, etc.), while others are due to differences in hereditary constitution. Generally both influences have been at work. The science of genetics suggests that hereditary differences between races have their basis in changes (mutations) in the elementary hereditary particles (genes). Differences in the frequencies of particular genes between different populations depend on the degree of reproductive isolation between them, and upon natural selection, fortuitous variation in gene frequency (genetic drift) and migration. The distribution of hereditary elements in populations is also affected by many social factors, such as marriage customs, which may produce partial reproductive isolation.

Race Mixture. Hereditary differences between races are constantly being broken down by intermarriage and crossing between members of different races. The evidence shows that this is a normal biological process which has been going on for a considerable time. There is no evidence that race mixture has disadvantageous biological effects and consequently there is no biological reason for prohibiting marriages between persons of different races.

New mixed populations, in so far as they in turn

become isolated geographically or socially, are subject to the same race-forming processes enumerated in Section 4 and these may lead to further changes.

Race Purity. There is no evidence that any so-called "pure" races exist today and, although our knowledge of the biology of extinct races is limited since derived chiefly from skeletal material, variability rather than uniformity seems to have been characteristic of all human populations.

The Races of Today. Existing races are merely the result, considered at a particular moment, of the total effect of the agencies of race formation and race mixture specified above.

Race and Mentality. Most anthropologists do not try to include mental characteristics in their classification of human races. Studies within a single race have shown that both innate capacity and environmental opportunity determine the results of tests of intelligence and temperament, though their relative importance is disputed.

The comparison of different races according to mental characters is beset with peculiar difficulties and hampered by incompleteness of knowledge of the heredity of normal psychological characteristics. With methods available at present it has never been possible to separate members of two racial groups on the basis of mental capacity. It is possible, though not proved, that special innate capacities may be commoner in one people than in another, in the same way as genes with effects on physical features have different frequencies in different racial groups. There is no evidence that differences between populations in innate capacity exceed the great variability found amongst members of the same population.

It often happens that a national group may appear to be characterized by particular psychological attributes. The superficial view would be that this is due to race. Scientifically, however, we realize that any common psychological attribute is more likely to be due to a common historical and social background, and that such attributes may obscure the fact that, within different

84

populations consisting of many human types, one will find the same range of temperament and intelligence.

Race and Culture. The scientific material available to us at present does not justify the conclusion that inherited genetic differences are a major factor in producing the differences between the cultures and cultural achievements of different peoples or groups. It does indicate, on the contrary, that the major factor in explaining such differences is the cultural experience which each group has undergone.

National, religious, geographical, linguistic and cultural groups do not necessarily coincide with racial groups; and the cultural traits of such groups have no demonstrated connexion with racial traits. The use of the term "race" in speaking of such groups is a serious error, but one which is habitually committed.

Vast social changes have occurred that have not been connected in any way with changes in racial type. Historical and sociological studies thus support the view that genetic differences are of little significance in determining the social and cultural differences between different groups of men.

Race and Equality. Equality of opportunity and equality at law in no way depend, as ethical principles, upon the assertion that human beings are in fact equal in endowment. The biological differences between human beings within a single race do not preclude the application of these principles, and since the biological differences between races are of similar kind and degree as those occurring within races, no biological reason exists for restricting in any way the principle of equality as applied to the races of man.

STATEMENT IN REPORT FORM: L. C. DUNN

The most noteworthy fact about the Statement is that it represents a large measure of agreement of just those specialists who are primarily concerned with the biology of race. Although students of special problems are likely to differ about the interpretation of scientific facts, there was no disagreement whatever about the point of primary importance, namely, that none of the evidence of biological difference between human groups seemed to these scientists to lend any support to doctrines of race inequality. All agreed that there were no scientific grounds for the racialist position which considers certain races as "pure" and establishes a hierarchy of superior and inferior races. There was agreement that all races were mixed and that the amount of biological variety within a race was as great as, if not greater than, the biological difference between races.

Concerning the meaning of race, there was complete agreement that it is properly used as a scientific term by which is meant a population which differs from other populations in some of its hereditary characters. These characters are those which can be observed and measured by the methods developed by anthropologists, supplemented by methods for describing characters, such as blood groups, which are not immediately visible. No one of the group believed that mental characters could be used in describing a race, and it was pointed out that in spite of frequent references in non-scientific literature to racial mentality, no serious student of race admits or uses such an idea.

Race is determined by biological heredity, by descent from particular parents and thus cannot properly be used to describe groups whose association is political (national), religious, or due to a community of language, or to other cultural or social factors, since these are not biologically inherited.

As is true of many other scientific terms of which the content changes as knowledge grows, the term "race" is not applied to particular cases by all scientists in precisely the same way. For those most closely concerned with the races of man, the physical anthropologists, races are categories required for classification of the varieties of mankind, and for arranging them in an order which may reveal their relationship and descent. The most reliable biological characters which have been used for classification have been physical ones such as dimensions of the body and the head, hair form, skin colour, and the like. But not all anthropologists agree as to the number of races that should be recognized by these criteria. Most of them agree on the distinctions between the larger groups, such as European, Asiatic, and African, but many of the subdivisions of these are difficult to distinguish. This is because of the great variability which is found within each race, leading to overlapping between races in a number of characters and consequently to uncertainty whether particular individuals should be classed as in one race or another. The difficulty is of course increased by the constantly occurring intermarriage between members of different races, as for example between Negroes and Europeans. Race mixture has been occurring on a large scale and for a long time and most "races" are probably "mixed" to a greater or lesser extent.

For students of heredity, geneticists, race has a double significance: first, for classifying groups of men according to their hereditary characters and, second, as a stage in the process by which populations become different from each other and adapted or fitted to the different environments in which they live. For geneticists a race is a group of people which has received from its ancestors a particular collection of hereditary elements (genes) and which has been enabled to retain this collection as somewhat different from other groups by the practice of contracting marriages prevailingly within the group.

Anthropologists in general recognize as races only those groups which are marked off from others by extensive physical differences, such as the native peoples of Africa, Europe and Asia. These are sometimes referred to as "major races" (*grand-races,* in French), but this term means only that the groups are large and show large physical differences from each other, probably owing to long continued geographical separation. It does not imply that there are "great" races and "less great" races.

Sociologists have sometimes referred to, as the "race problem", those tensions and conflicts which sometimes develop between members of different racial groups. Actually, of course, this problem is one of *race relations,* that is, a social question involving the causes of prejudice and conflict, and not the biological problem of what races are and how they form and change. The social problem as such was not dealt with by the anthropologists and geneticists; but the scientists agreed that none of the physical characters used in classifying races and tracing their descent could be regarded as giving any race inferior or superior status; and thus no scientific grounds exist for race prejudice or conflict referable to biological characters.

Although anthropologists can distinguish *groups* of people by their physical characters, they recognize that the great variability found within any group will often make it difficult to distinguish individual persons as belonging to this or that race. Races merge into each other in physical character, and the separation, especially of small neighbouring or related groups is seldom sharp. There is consequently much latitude for difference among anthropologists in the number of races to be recognized, and in the racial identification of particular races and particular individuals. Since classification is seldom an end in itself but generally serves some other purpose leading to a better understanding of human biology, it is quite understandable that there should be many schemes of classification at different times and for different purposes.

One peculiarity of all human populations lies at the bottom of the practical difficulties of racial classification and leads at the same time to the view of the nature of races which has become common amongst geneticists. All human groups show great variability in many bodily features. These bodily features are in general influenced by both heredity and environment; but even in similar environments a great deal of variability persists. This appears to be owing to the fact that there is a great variety of the elements of heredity, the genes. This variety has arisen in past ages by changes within the genes known as mutations. A gene representing straight hair may change to another form responsible for curliness of hair, and the new gene may continue to be transmitted in the same population with the old gene so that both curly and straight-haired people will be found in the population until such time as one gene proves to have some advantage over the other and replaces it. Mutations, although rare, are continually occurring, and different forms of genes are usually retained in the population unless they have very deleterious effects. Variability, once it starts, is maintained and increased by the usual custom of avoiding marriage between close relatives. This brings genes from different families and different parts of the population into new combinations and thus tends to make an enormous variety out of relatively few gene differences.

The conference recognized the importance of social factors which influence marriage customs and thus tend to keep certain genes within marriage groups such as those which are formed by religion, caste, or geographical isolation.

The history of human races seems to involve periods of relative isolation during which marriage within the group tends to conserve a collection of hereditary characters which differs somewhat from that possessed by neighbouring groups; but with the movements of people both ancient and modern these different collections tend to become fixed by intermarriage, and thus races or incipient races become merged until new isolating factors of whatever sort again come into operation.

The conference discussed at some length the evidence concerning the mixing of races, particularly whether it produced bad biological effects. There was entire agreement that such effects have never been demonstrated. The disadvantageous position which the children of mixed marriages sometimes have appears to be due to social not to biological factors. These can be improved by social change (elimination of prejudice, etc.). The cure does not lie in the prohibition of such marriages since there is no evidence that, of themselves, they produce bad effects. Several members of the conference thought that race mixture, in certain cases and perhaps generally, had beneficial effects in producing children of greater vigour than would appear from the same parents when married to members of their own race. But it was agreed the evidence was not sufficient to support this or any other conclusion at present.

Both the anthropological study of existing races and an examination of historical evidence led the conference to the view, now general amongst anthropologists and geneticists, that "pure" races do not exist and probably never have. This does not mean that races, as variable collections of hereditary characters differing somewhat from other populations, do not exist. It does mean that race is a dynamic not a static idea, a stage in the slow progress of change which occurs in all living populations as they become adjusted to the locally varying conditions of life. Races form as particular collections of hereditary elements; are conserved by geographical and social circumstances, and change as the collections are dispersed and lose their identity in other populations.

The question which gave the conference the most trouble and which it discussed for the longest time concerned mental differences. This was not because any modern anthropologist or geneticist ever uses mental characters in classifying races or studying the processes of race formation. This practice has had no scientific validity for a long time. The trouble arises from the difficulty of identifying and measuring mental characters which are so sensitive to the effects of such environmental factors as education and literacy, and from the difficulty of identifying the hereditary elements concerned with mental characters. Although it was recognized that in the absence of such methods and evidence based on them conclusions would be premature, still there was no hesitation in reaching essential agreement that variation in mental characters was at least as great within a race as between races, that is, that no two races appeared to differ as much *on the average* as the extreme variations found within a population. Although feeble-minded persons and idiots are found within practically every race, there are no feeble-minded or idiot races. Many scientists believe that there may be special innate capacities which occur more frequently in one race than in another, just as curly hair may be more frequent in one than in another. But even such conjectures cannot at present be tested by any reliable evidence. No member of the conference discerned any indication that mental characters could be used to limit the application of the principle of equality amongst races.

Many of the differences which appear to characterize races are due not to their biological inherited characters but to the effects of the society and culture in which they live. This is certainly true of groups united by nationality or religion or language which are clearly not racial; nor does residence in one country or neighbourhood produce of itself that community of hereditary element which follows long continued intramarriage. The greatest mistakes and abuses of the idea of race have been committed precisely by those who misunder-

90

stood this simple criterion that race is a *biological*, not a social or cultural concept. Nationality, language and religion may be changed in a single generation for any person or biological group or race; these cultural attributes of people do not depend in any way on biological endowment but on non-biological historical factors. The conference thought it could not be too strongly emphasized that race and culture arise from quite different origins and are affected by different factors. This is not to deny that social and cultural institutions may affect the formation or fusion of races; they do so however only through biological channels, that is, through influencing the ways in which hereditary characters are distributed within and between populations.

The final conclusions of this conference might have surprised le Comte de Gobineau, who just 100 years ago wrote his famous essay "Sur l'Inégalité des Races", but it could not come as a surprise to those who wrote the American Declaration of Independence or the Déclaration des Droits de l'Homme. The former document proposed to subordinate an ethical principle, equality, to what appeared to be a scientific fact, biological inequality and unlikeness amongst races. The latter declarations assumed equality as a condition of social existence which each man granted to his fellows in return for their recognition of his own personal right. The group of scientists meeting in 1951 agreed that none of the scientific evidence of the past 150 years provides any biological reason for limiting the principle of equality as applied to races.

PHYSICAL ANTHROPOLOGISTS AND GENETICISTS INVITED TO COMMENT UPON THE STATEMENT [1]

ACKERKNECHT, Professor Erwin E., Department of History of Medicine, University of Wisconsin Medical School, Madison, Wis., U.S.A.

*ANGEL, Professor J. Lawrence, Baugh Institute of Anatomy, Jefferson Medical College, Philadelphia, Pa., U.S.A.

*BARIGOZZI, Dr. C., University of Milano, Italy.

BEAGLEHOLE, Professor Ernest, Victoria University College, Wellington, New Zealand.

BELTRAN, Professor Enrique, Instituto de Investigaciónes Scientíficas, Universidad de Nuevo Leon, Monterrey, N.L., Mexico.

BIRCH, Dr. L. C., Department of Zoology, University of Sydney, Australia.

BIRDSELL, Professor Joseph B., Department of Anthropology and Sociology, University of California, Los Angeles, Cal., U.S.A.

*BOYD, Professor William C., University School of Medicine, Boston, Mass., U.S.A.

*BURKITT, Professor A. St. N., Department of Anatomy, University of Sydney, Australia.

BUZZATI-TRAVERSO, Professor Adriano, Instituto di Genetica, University of Pavia, Italy.

CASTLE, Professor W. E., Division of Genetics, College of Agriculture, University of California, Berkeley, Cal., U.S.A.

CHATTOPADHYAY, Professor K. P., Department of Anthropology, University of Calcutta, India.

CLARK, Professor W. E. Le Gros, Department of Human Anatomy, University of Oxford, England.

CLARKE, Dr. Hans T., Science Attaché, American Embassy, London.

COMAS, Professor Juan, Escuela Nacional de Antropología, Mexico.

1. Names preceded by an asterisk are those of anthropologists or geneticists from whom no comments were received.

CONNOLLY, Father Cornelius J., Department of Anthropology, The Catholic University of America, Washington, D.C., U.S.A.

COON, Professor Carleton S., University Museum, Philadelphia, Pa., U.S.A.

CUNHA, Dr. A. Brito da, Departamento de Biologia Geral, University of São Paulo, Brazil.

DARLINGTON, Dr. C. D., John Innes Horticultural Institution, Bayfordbury, Herts, England.

*DAVID, Professor Paul, Department of Zoology, University of Oklahoma, Norman, Okla., U.S.A.

DREYFUS, (The late), Professor André, Departamento de Biologia Geral, University of São Paulo, Brazil.

EICKSTEDT, Professor Egon Von, University of Mainz, Germany.

*EPHRUSSI, Professor Boris, Institut de Biologie, University of Paris.

FISCHER, Professor Eugen, University of Freiburg i./Br., Germany.

FISHER, Professor Sir Ronald, Department of Genetics, University of Cambridge, England.

*FORD, Professor E. B., Department of Zoology and Comparative Anatomy, University of Oxford, England.

FRANKEL, Dr. Otto H., Group Research Division, Department of Scientific and Industrial Research, Lincoln, New Zealand.

*FROE, Professor A. de, Department of Anthropology, University of Amsterdam, Netherlands.

FROTA-PESSOA, Professor Oswaldo, Faculdade Nacional de Filosofia, Universidade do Brasil, Rio de Janeiro.

*GAZIC, Professor Gabriel, Universidad Nacional de Chile, Santiago de Chile.

GENNA, Professor Giuseppe, Director, Istituto di Antropologia, University of Florence, Italy.

*GLASS, Professor H. Bentley, Department of Biology, Johns Hopkins University, Baltimore, Md., U.S.A.

GRÜNEBERG, Dr. Hans, Department of Genetics, University College, London.

GUSINDE, Father Martin, The Catholic University of America, Washington, D.C.

HEIDELBERGER, Dr. Michael, Department of Medicine, College of Physicians and Surgeons, Columbia University, New York.

HERSKOVITS, Professor Melville J., Department of Anthropology, Northwestern University, Evanston, Ill., U.S.A.

*HOGBEN, Professor Lancelot, Department of Medical Statistics, Queen Elizabeth Hospital, University of Birmingham, England.

*HOOTON, Professor Earnest A., Department of Anthropology, Harvard University, Cambridge, Mass., U.S.A.

HOWELLS, Professor William W., Department of Sociology and Anthropology, University of Wisconsin, Madison, Wis., U.S.A.

HUXLEY, Dr. Julian, 31 Pond Street, Hampstead, London.

ILTIS, Professor Hugo, Department of Biology and Genetics, Mary Washington College, University of Virginia, Fredericksburg, Va., U.S.A.

*JONES, Dr. Neville, National Museum of Southern Rhodesia, Bulawayo, Southern Rhodesia.

KABIR, Dr. Humayun, Ministry of Education, New Delhi, India.

KEMP, Professor T., University Institute for Human Genetics, Copenhagen, Denmark.

KOMAI, Professor Taku, National Institute of Genetics, Misima, Sizuoka-Ken, Japan.

KROGMAN, Professor Wilton Marion, Graduate School of Medicine, University of Pennsylvania, Philadelphia, Pa., U.S.A.

LANDAUER, Professor Walter, Storrs Agricultural Experiment Station, University of Connecticut, Storrs, Conn., U.S.A.

LENZ, Professor F., Institut für Menschliche Erblehre, University of Göttingen, Germany.

LIPSCHUTZ, Professor A., Director, Departamento de Medicina Experimental, Dirección General de Sanidad, Santiago de Chile.

LURIA, Professor S. E., Department of Bacteriology, University of Illinois, Urbana, Ill., U.S.A.

*MALINOWSKI, Professor E., Institute of Genetics, Skierniewice, Poland.

MATHER, Professor Kenneth, Department of Genetics, University of Birmingham, England.

MAYR, Dr. Ernst, Department of Zoology, American Museum of Natural History, New York.

*McCown, Professor T. D., Department of Anthropology, University of California, Berkeley, Cal., U.S.A.

Mirsky, Dr. A. E., Rockefeller Institute for Medical Research, New York.

Mohr, Professor Otto L., Rector, University of Norway, Oslo.

Morant, Dr. G. M., Farnborough, Hampshire, England.

*Moriwaki, Professor D., Department of Biology, Faculty of Science, Tokyo Metropolitan University, Tokyo, Japan.

Muller, Professor H. J., Department of Zoology, Indiana University, Bloomington, Ind., U.S.A.

Needham, Dr. Joseph, Department of Biochemistry, University of Cambridge, England.

Neel, Dr. James V., Heredity Clinic, University of Michigan, Ann Arbor, Mich., U.S.A.

*Neumann, Dr. George K., Department of Anthropology, Indiana University, Bloomington, Ind., U.S.A.

Newman, Dr. Marshall T., Curator, Division of Physical Anthropology, Smithsonian Institution, Washington, D.C.

Park, Professor Thomas, Department of Zoology, University of Chicago, Ill., U.S.A.

*Parshley, Professor H. M., Smith College, Northampton, Mass., U.S.A.

Penrose, Professor L. S., Galton Laboratory, University College, London.

*Pittard, Professor Eugène, Director, Musée d'Ethnographie, Geneva, Switzerland.

Reed, Professor Sheldon C., Director, The Dight Institute for Human Genetics, University of Minnesota, Minneapolis, Minn., U.S.A.

*Remmelts, Professor R., Instituut voor Praeventieve Geneeskunde, University of Leiden, Netherlands.

*Rostand, Dr. Jean, Section de Biologie, Palais de la Découverte, Paris.

Saller, Professor Karl Felix, Anthropologisches Institut, University of Munich, Germany.

*Sander, Dr. Gerhard, Department of Botany, University of Wisconsin, Madison, Wis., U.S.A.

Sauter, Professor M.-R., Institut d'Anthropologie, University of Geneva, Switzerland.

Sax, Professor Karl, Biological Laboratories, Harvard University, Cambridge, Mass., U.S.A.

SCHEIDT, Professor Walter, Director, Anthropologisches Institut, University of Hamburg, Germany.

*SCHLAGINHAUFEN, Professor Otto, Anthropologisches Institut, University of Zürich, Switzerland.

SCHULTZ, Professor Adolph H., Director, Anthropologisches Institut, University of Zürich, Switzerland.

*SINNOTT, Professor Edmund W., Osborn Botanical Laboratory, Yale University, New Haven, Conn., U.S.A.

SKERLJ, Professor Bozo, Director, Anthropological Institute, University of Ljubljana, Yugoslavia.

SNYDER, Professor Laurence H., Dean, Graduate College, University of Oklahoma, Norman, Okla., U.S.A.

STEINBERG, Dr. Arthur G., Division of Biometry and Medical Statistics, Mayo Clinic, Rochester, Minn., U.S.A.

STEINMANN, Professor Alfred B., Vice-President, Société Suisse d'Anthropologie et d'Ethnologie, Zürich, Switzerland.

STERN, Professor Curt, Department of Zoology, University of California, Berkeley, Cal., U.S.A.

STEWART, Dr. T. Dale, Curator, Division of Physical Anthropology, Smithsonian Institution, Washington, D.C.

STURTEVANT, Professor A. H., Kerckoff Laboratories of Biology, California Institute of Technology, Pasadena, Cal., U.S.A.

SUMMERS, Dr. Roger, Curator, National Museum of Southern Rhodesia, Bulawayo.

*TAMAGNINI, Professor E., Instituto de Antropologia, University of Coimbra, Portugal.

TEILHARD DE CHARDIN, Rev. Father Pierre, Institut de Paleontologie humaine, Paris.

*TEISSIER, Professor Georges, Director, Laboratoire de Zoologie, University of Paris.

TILDESLEY, Miss M. L., Croxley Green, Hertfordshire, England.

WADDINGTON, Professor C. H., Institute of Animal Genetics, University of Edinburgh, Scotland.

WASHBURN, Professor S. L., Department of Anthropology, University of Chicago, Ill., U.S.A.

WEINERT, Professor Hans, Director, Anthropologisches Institut, University of Kiel, Germany.

WENINGER, Professor Josef, Director, Anthropologisches Institut, University of Vienna, Austria.

WILSON, Professor Monica, School of African Studies, University of Cape Town, South Africa.

*WRIGHT, Professor Sewal, Hull Zoological Laboratory, University of Chicago, Ill., U.S.A.

APPENDIX

Text of the Statement of 1950

1. Scientists have reached general agreement in recognizing that mankind is one: that all men belong to the same species, *Homo sapiens*. It is further generally agreed among scientists that all men are probably derived from the same common stock; and that such differences as exist between different groups of mankind are due to the operation of evolutionary factors of differentiation such as isolation, the drift and random fixation of the material particles which control heredity (the genes), changes in the structure of these particles, hybridization, and natural selection. In these ways groups have arisen of varying stability and degree of differentiation which have been classified in different ways for different purposes.

2. From the biological standpoint, the species *Homo sapiens* is made up of a number of populations, each one of which differs from the others in the frequency of one or more genes. Such genes, responsible for the hereditary differences between men, are always few when compared to the whole genetic constitution of man and to the vast number of genes common to all human beings regardless of the population to which they belong. This means that the likenesses among men are far greater than their differences.

3. A race, from the biological standpoint, may therefore be defined as one of the group of populations constituting the species *Homo sapiens*. These populations are capable of interbreeding with one another but, by virtue of the isolating barriers which in the past kept them more or less separated, exhibit certain physical differences as a result of their somewhat different biological histories. These represent variations, as it were, on a common theme.

4. In short, the term "race" designates a group or population characterized by some concentrations, relative as to frequency and distribution, of hereditary particles (genes) or physical characters, which appear, fluctuate, and often disappear in the course of time by reason of geographic and/or cultural isolation. The varying manifestations of these traits in different populations are perceived in different ways by each group. What is perceived is largely preconceived, so that each group arbitrarily tends to misinterpret the variability which occurs as a fundamental difference which separates that group from all others.

5. These are the scientific facts. Unfortunately, however, when most people use the term "race" they do not do so in the sense above defined. To most people, a race is any group of people whom they choose to describe as a race. Thus, many national, religious, geographic, linguistic or cultural groups have, in such loose usage, been called "race", when obviously Americans are not a race, nor are Englishmen, nor Frenchmen, nor any other national group. Catholics, Protestants, Moslems and Jews are not races, nor are groups who speak English or any other language thereby definable as a race; people who live in Iceland or England or India are not races; nor are people who are culturally Turkish or Chinese or the like thereby describable as races.

6. National, religious, geographic, linguistic and cultural groups do not necessarily coincide with racial groups; and the cultural traits of such groups have no demonstrated genetic connexion with racial traits. Because serious errors of this kind are habitually committed when the term "race" is used in popular parlance, it would be better when speaking of human races to drop the term "race" altogether and speak of *ethnic groups*.

7. Now what has the scientist to say about the groups of mankind which may be recognized at the present time? Human races can be and have been differently classified by different anthropologists, but at the present time most anthropologists agree on classifying the greater part of present-day mankind into three major

99

divisions, as follows: the Mongoloid Division, the Negroid Division, the Caucasoid Division. The biological processes which the classifier has here embalmed, as it were, are dynamic, not static. These divisions were not the same in the past as they are at present, and there is every reason to believe that they will change in the future.

8. Many sub-groups or ethnic groups within these divisions have been described. There is no general agreement upon their number, and in any event most ethnic groups have not yet been either studied or described by the physical anthropologists.

9. Whatever classification the anthropologist makes of man, he never includes mental characteristics as part of those classifications. It is now generally recognized that intelligence tests do not in themselves enable us to differentiate safely between what is due to innate capacity and what is the result of environmental influences, training and education. Wherever it has been possible to make allowances for differences in environmental opportunities, the tests have shown essential similarity in mental characters among all human groups. In short, given similar degrees of cultural opportunity to realize their potentialities, the average achievement of the members of each ethnic group is about the same. The scientific investigations of recent years fully support the dictum of Confucius (551-478 B.C.): "Men's natures are alike; it is their habits that carry them far apart."

10. The scientific material available to us at present does not justify the conclusion that inherited genetic differences are a major factor in producing the differences between the cultures and cultural achievements of different peoples or groups. It does indicate, however, that the history of the cultural experience which each group has undergone is the major factor in explaining such differences. The one trait which above all others has been at a premium in the evolution of men's mental characters has been educability, plasticity. This is a trait which all human beings possess. It is indeed, a species character of *Homo sapiens*.

11. So far as temperament is concerned, there is no definite evidence that there exist inborn differences between human groups. There is evidence that whatever group differences of the kind there might be are greatly over-ridden by the individual differences, and by the differences springing from environmental factors.

12. As for personality and character, these may be considered raceless. In every human group a rich variety of personality and character types will be found, and there is no reason for believing that any human group is richer than any other in these respects.

13. With respect to race-mixture, the evidence points unequivocally to the fact that this has been going on from the earliest times. Indeed, one of the chief processes of race-formation and race-extinction or absorption is by means of hybridization between races or ethnic groups. Furthermore, no convincing evidence has been adduced that race-mixture of itself produces biologically bad effects. Statements that human hybrids frequently show undesirable traits, both physically and mentally, physical disharmonies and mental degeneracies, are not supported by the facts. There is, therefore, no "biological" justification for prohibiting intermarriage between persons of different ethnic groups.

14. The biological fact of race and the myth of "race" should be distinguished. For all practical social purposes "race" is not so much a biological phenomenon as a social myth. The myth "race" has created an enormous amount of human and social damage. In recent years it has taken a heavy toll in human lives and caused untold suffering. It still prevents the normal development of millions of human beings and deprives civilization of the effective co-operation of productive minds. The biological differences between ethnic groups should be disregarded from the standpoint of social acceptance and social action. The unity of mankind from both the biological and social viewpoints is the main thing. To recognize this and to act accordingly is the first requirement of modern man. It is but to recognize what a great biologist wrote in 1875: "As man advances in civilization, and small tribes are united into larger

communities, the simplest reason would tell each individual that he ought to extend his social instincts and sympathies to all the members of the same nation, though personally unknown to him. This point being once reached, there is only an artificial barrier to prevent his sympathies extending to the men of all nations and races." These are the words of Charles Darwin in *The Descent of Man* (2nd ed., 1875, pp. 187-88). And, indeed, the whole of human history shows that a co-operative spirit is not only natural to men, but more deeply rooted than any self-seeking tendencies. If this were not so we should not see the growth of integration and organization of his communities which the centuries and the millenia plainly exhibit.

15. We now have to consider the bearing of these statements on the problem of human equality. It must be asserted with the utmost emphasis that equality as an ethical principle in no way depends upon the assertion that human beings are in fact equal in endowment. Obviously individuals in all ethnic groups vary greatly among themselves in endowment. Nevertheless, the characteristics in which human groups differ from one another are often exaggerated and used as a basis for questioning the validity of equality in the ethical sense. For this purpose we have thought it worth while to set out in a formal manner what is at present scientifically established concerning individual and group differences.

(a) In matters of race, the only characteristics which anthropologists can effectively use as a basis for classifications are physical and physiological.

(b) According to present knowledge there is no proof that the groups of mankind differ in their innate mental characteristics, whether in respect of intelligence or temperament. The scientific evidence indicates that the range of mental capacities in all ethnic groups is much the same.

(c) Historical and sociological studies support the view that genetic differences are not of importance in determining the social and cultural differences between different groups of *Homo sapiens,* and that the social and cultural *changes* in different groups have, in the main, been independent of *changes* in inborn constitution. Vast social changes have occured which were not in any way connected with changes in racial type.

(d) There is no evidence that race-mixture as such produces bad results from the biological point of view. The social results of race-mixture whether for good or ill are to be traced to social factors.

(e) All normal human beings are capable of learning to share in a common life, to understand the nature of mutual service and reciprocity, and to respect social obligations and contracts. Such biological differences as exist between members of different ethnic groups have no relevance to problems of social and political organization, moral life and communication between human beings.

Lastly, biological studies lend support to the ethic of universal brotherhood; for man is born with drives toward co-operation, and unless these drives are satisfied, men and nations alike fall ill. Man is born a social being who can reach his fullest development only through interaction with his fellows. The denial at any point of this social bond between man and man brings with it disintegration. In this sense, every man is his brother's keeper. For every man is a piece of the continent, a part of the main, because he is involved in mankind.

The original statement was drafted at Unesco House, Paris by the following experts:

Professor Ernest Beaglehole, New Zealand;
Professor Juan Comas, Mexico;
Professor L. A. Costa Pinto, Brazil;
Professor E. Franklin Frazier, United States of America;
Professor Morris Ginsberg, United Kingdom;
Dr. Humayun Kabir, India;
Professor Claude Levi-Strauss, France;
Professor M. F. Ashley-Montagu, United States of America (Rapporteur).

The text was revised by Professor Ashley-Montagu, after criticisms submitted by Professors Hadley Cantril, E. G. Conklin, Gunnar Dahlberg, Theodosius Dobzhansky, L. C. Dunn, Donald Hager, Julian S. Huxley, Otto Klineberg, Wilbert Moore, H. J. Muller, Gunnar Myrdal, Joseph Needham, Curt Stern.